Before They Were SEALs They Were Frogs

Before They Were SEALs They Were Frogs

The Story of the Lone Surviving Member of Class 1 of Naval Special Warfare Operators Who Evolved into Navy SEALs

By William "Bill" Dawson

With Tom Hawkins and Lisa Merriam

Before They Were SEALs They Were Frogs

www.PhocaPress.com

"Freddy and Sammy" illustration by Lowell Gosser, former Chief Petty Officer in SEAL Team TWO

PHOCA
Press ✦ LLC

Published by Phoca Press
New York, NY 10025
www.PhocaPress.com

Phoca Press publishes works by, for, and about Naval Special Warfare. Our mission is to enhance the public's appreciation and understanding of the contributions of the Naval Special Warfare community through history up to today.

ISBN-13: 978-0-9909153-2-4

10 9 8 7 6 5 4 3 2

For my friends and brothers in Class 1

Table of Contents

"It is not the critic who counts, not the man who points out how the strong man stumbled, or where the doer of deeds could have done better. The credit belongs to the man who is actually in the arena; whose face is marred by the dust and sweat and blood; who strives valiantly; who errs and comes short again and again; who knows the great enthusiasms, the great devotions and spends himself in a worthy course; who at the best, knows in the end the triumph of high achievement, and who, at worst, if he fails, at least fails while daring greatly; so that his place shall never be with those cold and timid souls who know neither victory or defeat."

Theodore Roosevelt (Paris Sorbonne, 1910)

An Extraordinary Account of Extraordinary Men

This is the extraordinary account of an extraordinary group of men who served together for over two and one-half years in various locations throughout the Pacific Theater of Operations during World War II.

Bill Dawson was a young man who grew up in Washington, DC during the 1930s depression. His story begins as he emerged into adulthood, and as the country was expanding its involvement in separate wars throughout the Pacific and Europe—World War II. Bill and his teammates became a part of the "greatest generation," but they didn't know it at the time.

Presented through the eyes and memory of William "Bill" Dawson, this is the fascinating and enduring story of one of the graduates of the first class of Naval Combat Demolition Unit warriors, a legacy organization that evolved into modern-day U.S. Navy SEALs.

I am a retired Navy SEAL Commander with 24 years of active service with the teams. I have known Bill for decades, and have always looked forward to seeing him at various SEAL reunions. I have long been fascinated by his binder, six inches thick, of photographs and memorabilia of his time in the service. I knew what I was seeing was a unique collection of great value. Lisa Merriam and I are dedicated to telling the story of Naval Special Warfare, and we are honored to present Bill's extraordinary collection and narrative to the general public.

Commander Tom Hawkins, USN, [Ret.]

Forward by Admiral Eric T. Olson, U.S. Navy, (Retired)

Today's Navy SEALs inherited their legacy from the brave warriors who pioneered commando operations in and around the sea. In World War II, the need for extraordinary troopers to conduct dangerous missions in the harshest of environments was especially compelling, and several nations at war formed small and highly specialized teams of such men.

In the United States, these teams were the OSS Maritime Unit, the Navy Scouts and Raiders, Navy Combat Demolition Units and Navy Underwater Demolition Teams. The members of the NCDUs and UDTs, "naked warriors" at the time and later "frogmen" because of their appearance in green rubber suits, daringly surveyed beaches, demolished reefs and exploded underwater obstacles to open lanes for amphibious assault craft. In the Southwest Pacific, small NCDUs moved from island to island in support of General MacArthur's landing forces. With one officer and five enlisted men in each team, often operating under enemy fire, they were essential elements in hard-fought campaigns.

Young Bill Dawson was one of these men, an original member of the NCDUs, and his personal story is one of courage, wide-eyed adventure, teammates in combat and innocent humility. He tells it straight from his gut, unembellished and supported by his diary and scrapbook. Not yet 20 years old when the war ended, his view of the operations was through a fresh lens – and his presentation of it is raw, candid, sometimes humorous, always inspirational. The reality that my professional experience is connected to his is a source of profound pride.

In his later years, Bill took up the hobby of crafting items out of leather. I now carry my keys on a leather fob that he gave to me several years ago. Stamped into one side is the now-famous "Trident" insignia of a Navy SEAL. I keep it as symbol of the Brotherhood of the Teams – transcending time, distance and the nature of war.

We all owe much to Bill Dawson and the dauntless men with whom he served. They were important to the outcome of World War II, for sure, but even more so were they the models for today's most capable and accomplished military forces. The tales of modern-day SEALs are hard to miss, but stories like Bill Dawson's are very much worth seeking out.

Eric Olson is a retired United States Navy Admiral who served as the commander of the U.S. Special Operations Cpmmand (USSOCOM) from 2007-2011. He was the first SEAL officer to be promoted to three-star and four-star ranks.

Chapter 1
Nothing Extraordinary about My Childhood

I was born in the Southeast section Washington, DC April 18, 1925. My dad was William A. Dawson and my mother was Elizabeth Howard Dawson. I had one sister, Ruth.

The only picture I have of my mother was taken under a cherry tree at the Tidal Basin in Washington, DC when I was about four years old.

I grew up during the Great Depression. My mother was a homemaker and my father was a motion picture operator. We felt fortunate that he had a good job. He worked hard to provide for us and was the first to volunteer for spare work if someone wanted a day off. I believe he worked in every theater in Washington at one time or another. I was pretty popular with my friends, because, when he was working, I could get us in to movies for free.

I was an athlete in school and did well in football and basketball. Back then, I was tall and lanky with a muscular build. I had a cheerful outlook on life. I never had a problem when it came to girls. I have to say, not much has changed in that regard, though I don't have the same physique. I had a happy time growing up, despite the troubles in the world. There was nothing extraordinary about my childhood that could have foretold what I was about to encounter.

After finishing at Chamberlin Vocational High School, I didn't really know what I wanted to do. I had several small jobs as I began seeking direction for my future life.

Events took over planning for me. I was working a full-time job at the Washington Navy Yard and was there on December 7, 1941, the day Japan bombed Pearl Harbor. The Navy Yard was a flood of activity, as we raced to get on war footing.

At that time, the Navy Yard was home to the largest naval ordnance plant in the world—pretty ironic, given my future career involving massive quantities of explosives!

During 1943, the war had expanded in Europe. The United States was allied with England and France to defeat Nazi Germany and fascists Italy. It had truly become a World War of unequaled proportions, and the United States was squarely in the middle of it. Young men around Bill's age were aware that war had broken out in the Pacific and Europe. The news was covered extensively in the *Washington Post, Times-Herald*, and *Evening Star* newspapers; broadcast continuously on WSJV radio; and could be seen in every movie theater, where Movietone newsreels played before each featured film. Media vividly displayed the actions and activities on the war front like they had never been seen before.

Suddenly the war was everywhere. While most people saw small changes with rationing and putting up black-out curtains, I had a different perspective.

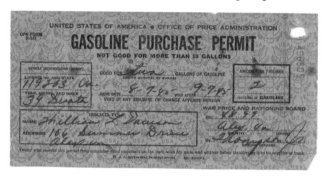

Working in the Navy Yard, I had a front row seat to our preparations. After a few months, I got to feeling I could be of more help by enlisting.

Just days before my birthday, on April 14, 1943, I took a day off of work and joined the Navy. Most guys signed on "for the duration plus six months." Because I was still seventeen, I qualified for a "minority cruise," which meant I was only required to serve until I turned twenty-one.

The only picture I have of my mother is when we were visiting the cherry blossoms around the Tidal Basin a few minutes from where we lived. I was four years old, and was wearing a white Navy sailor suit that day, so I guess it stuck with me. You could say I had liked the Navy nearly all my life. Ironically, those cherry trees were a gift from the Mayor of Tokyo commemorating the friendship between the United States and Japan.

Here I am in my Navy uniform shortly after enlisting with my childhood friend Ray Roberts.

Before I knew it, I was headed north to the Naval Training Center in Bainbridge, Maryland on the Susquehanna River. I had a brand new camera in my duffel bag.

In the back yard of my house in Southeast Washington,
DC before heading to NCDU training

Quite often men in uniform, who had not yet shipped out, would be called on to participate in various ceremonies around town. I don't remember this specific event—there were a lot of them—but I do remember having a good time with my friends and making my parents proud.

Chapter 2
Sneaking In and Surviving Training

I entered boot camp at Bainbridge, Maryland in April, 1943. Our days were filled with drilling and calisthenics. Sometimes they would have us form "human pictures" and pose for aerial images to use on patriotic postcards. We also learned military bearing, including how to care for and wear our uniforms.

For reasons I can't recall, I had a strong desire for submarine duty. Before graduating from boot camp, however, I discovered an assignment to submarines would not be possible. All of the spots for submarine duty had been filled. This was truly bad timing for me and I was terribly disappointed. I needed to make another choice pretty fast.

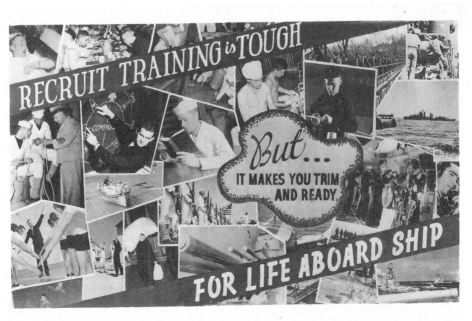

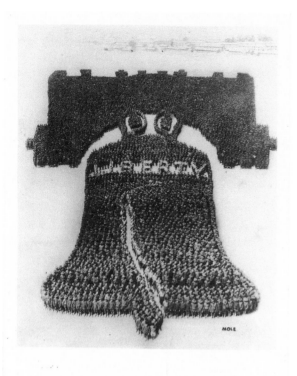

The Human Liberty Bell
U.S. NAVAL TRAINING STATION
BAINBRIDGE, MARYLAND

Human Statue of Liberty
U.S. NAVAL TRAINING STATION
BAINBRIDGE, MARYLAND

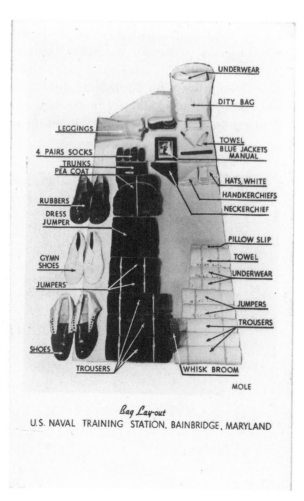

Bag Lay-out
U.S. NAVAL TRAINING STATION, BAINBRIDGE, MARYLAND

The Human American Eagle

U.S. NAVAL
TRAINING
STATION

BAINBRIDGE,
MARYLAND

Bags Laid Out

U.S. NAVAL

TRAINING

STATION

BAINBRIDGE,

MARYLAND

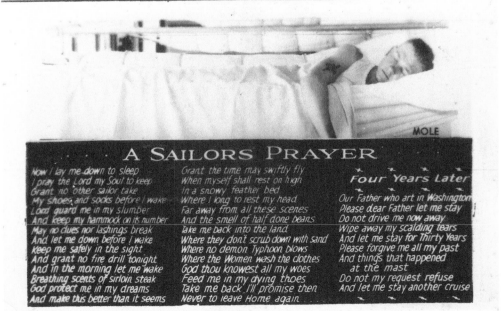

A SAILORS PRAYER

Now I lay me down to sleep
I pray the Lord my Soul to keep
Grant no other sailor take
My shoes and socks before I wake
Lord guard me in my slumber
And keep my hammock on its number
May no clues nor lashings break
And let me down before I wake
Keep me safely in the sight
And grant no fire drill tonight
And in the morning let me wake
Breathing scents of sirloin steak
God protect me in my dreams
And make this better than it seems

Grant the time may swiftly fly
When myself shall rest on high
In a snowy feather bed
Where I long to rest my head
Far away from all these scenes
And the smell of half done beans
Take me back into the land
Where they don't scrub down with sand
Where no demon Typhoon blows
Where the Women wash the clothes
God thou knowest all my woes
Feed me in my dying thoes
Take me back. I'll promise then
Never to leave Home again.

Four Years Later

Our Father who art in Washington
Please dear Father let me stay
Do not drive me now away
Wipe away my scalding tears
And let me stay for Thirty Years
Please forgive me all my past
And things that happened
at the mast
Do not my request refuse
And let me stay another cruise

While lazing around the barracks one evening, one of my buddies told me that there was a presentation in the base theater. They were looking for volunteers for distant and hazardous duty that involved blowing things up. That sounded interesting! I had no better idea of what I wanted to do, so I went over with several of my shipmates to find out more.

What Bill didn't know was that the Chief of Naval Operations had sent out an urgent fleet-wide directive to establish permanent Naval Combat Demolition Units (NCDUs) for the Atlantic Fleet. Naval Combat Demolition Units were created on 6 June 1943, with a training school established at Fort Pierce, Florida under the leadership of LCDR Draper Kauffman.

When we got to the base theater, the doors were closed. A gruff fellow in front of the door told us they already had over 500 guys in there and they were not letting anyone else in.

My friend and I badly wanted to get out of Bainbridge, so we did not take "no" for an answer. We went to the back of the building and stacked up some crates. We climbed up on them so we could crawl in through the window. We slipped into the line of applicants like we belonged there. We didn't know what we were getting into, but we were able to confirm that we would get to learn how to blow things up. That was the important part!

Of the hundreds of men who applied, my friend and I were among the 42 men selected that day for this new, not-yet-named unit.

Next thing you know, we found ourselves bound for Fort Pierce, Florida and training for Naval Combat Demolition Units—NCDUs.

When we got off the train, we boarded a truck that took us to a brand new base. It was so new there were no buildings at all; just a tent city surrounded by thick, sub-tropical growth. Row upon row of tents were pitched on the sand just over the dunes from the open ocean. We would come to find out that they didn't even have water, which was trucked in every day. Fort Pierce

Metropolis Of The Indian River

"Fort Pierce"

(Photo by Fla. Photographic Concern)

was a whole lot of nothing. We had an endless supply of mosquitoes and sand fleas. I was about to get very well acquainted with those.

It didn't take long for us to realize what we were in for. With few introductions, we were mustered and formed into working parties to erect five-man tents for ourselves on the barren sand. Home was a pole and canvas; we didn't get the luxury of wood flooring until much later.

Mess hall was another one of those luxuries we did without. We subsisted on powdered eggs, dehydrated potatoes, and K-rations that cooks prepared in a dedicated kitchen tent. The "dining hall" consisted of tables and benches out in the open air, which we shared with the mosquitos and sand fleas. We dined on powdered food and they dined on us.

In June 1943, Bill found himself and hundreds of other men on a train heading south to Florida. In a short time, they arrived at a place called Fort Pierce on the Atlantic Ocean. Bill was soon to learn that he was among 98 officer and enlisted volunteers taken from the Seabee training facility at Camp Peary, Virginia and the Bomb and Mine Disposal School in Washington, DC to begin this training. He also learned that he was one of only a few taken directly from the boot camp at Bainbridge.

At night, we erected mosquito netting around ourselves that offered little protection. For the most part, the sand fleas and mosquitoes had their way with us. The mosquito and sand flea problem was so bad, they didn't even try to control it. I often said I wanted

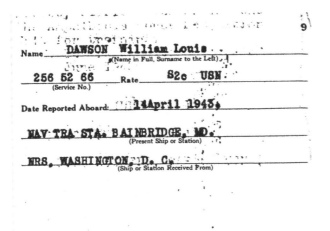

Me in typical sleeping attire out by the water truck—we didn't have plumbing on the base.

to lie down and cry it was so bad, but the mosquitos would not let me. Sometimes it felt like they lifted me up and kept me going.

Once we got our section of the new base organized, training began in earnest. We were formed into groups of one officer and five enlisted men. This was the size of the six-man boat crew that manned the 350 pound inflatable rubber boats we used for training. The groups also determined the size of each numbered NCDU. We gave our groups nicknames, mostly based on the name of our commanding officer, such as "Jeeter's Skeeters" or "Shinner's Bathtub Sailors." I was a proud member of "Kaine's Killers," with Lieutenant Junior Grade Frank Kaine in charge.

I had a picture taken when I got to Fort Pierce to send home.

At first, the groups were not stable. Many men quit during training. The program was a lot more demanding than we expected, and many men simply did not want to or could not endure it.

Training began at five a.m. each morning with a three-and-a-half mile run around palm trees, through soft sand, and many trips across a rock jetty at the

entrance to the bay. That jetty was covered with slippery algae, wet with ocean wash. The jetty eliminated a number of the men, who ended up with broken bones

Overall initial physical training for the NCDU School was provided entirely by U.S. Army Sergeants from the Scout and Raider School. Scouts and Raiders were a joint Army-Navy pre-assault commando force formed at Amphibious Training Base, Little Creek, Norfolk, Virginia in August 1942. At Little Creek they trained and prepared to conduct operations and activities for Opertion TORCH, which was the invasion of North Africa conducted the following November. The training school was moved to the Fort Pierce base in February 1943, with veterans from the Africa operations. These were combat-experienced sailors and soldiers, and no doubt these sergeants enjoyed putting Navy NCDU "swabbies" through a torturous pace.

Swimming in the ocean off Fort Pierce—the water could be remarkably calm sometimes.

Our rubber boat was our ubiquitous companion.

after falling on or between the rocks, or who quit for fear of future injury.

After the run, we had thirty minutes of vigorous calisthenics followed by breakfast. Then the real work began. Our days usually stretched to eighteen hours of training because they wanted to get us out to the fleet in a hurry. The sergeants that trained us tried to put us through the ropes and did a good job of it. It was pretty much in and out of the water all the time. We had to carry our rubber boats everywhere we went. We paddled them when we were in the water. And when we were on land, we carried those 350 pound boats on our shoulders or over our heads.

Much to my amazement, all of the officers and enlisted men trained together side-by-side. The training was pretty tough, but I was only eighteen and an athlete, so I took right to it. The officers were older, maybe twenty-five or thirty years old. They did a great

EX. HOSE

A pair of us on the beach at Fort Pierce walking past stacks of explosive hose, holding spools of electrical cord in our hands.

25

job of keeping up with the younger men and some of the younger men could not keep up with them.

What amazed me most was that Commander Kaufman, the head of the whole outfit, trained right with us whenever he was not in Washington. He sure earned our respect for that. We didn't mind it when we heard him talking about us during training. He was explaining to a visiting observer about telescoping eight weeks of training into seven days for a week that was meant to separate the men from the boys. The trouble was, he said: "The men had sense enough to quit—leaving us with the boys!"

We knew LCDR Kaufmann was catching a lot of flak for making the training too tough. Since he went through it personally himself and survived it, he was able to shut down the critics.

We trained on all sorts of obstacle courses and also did weeks of the now-famous log PT. I have scars on my arms I could show you today that I got from throwing logs back and forth to the other men in training.

We did a lot of crawling through the brush down there. I vividly recall getting cut up by plants with

1825—Captain Clarence Gulbranson, U. S. N., Commanding Officer, Fort Pierce, Florida.

1826—Captain Clarence Gulbranson, U. S. N., Commanding Officer, conducts an inspection at Fort Pierce, Florida.

1827—Rubber Assault Boat Crews at Fort Pierce, Florida.

1820—L. C. V. P. (Landing Craft, Vehicle-Personnel), Fort Pierce, Florida.

I picked up a number of postcards to share with my family, so they could get some idea of what we were doing at Fort Pierce. Our training was considered top secret. Individuals were discouraged from taking photographs; not that we had the time or energy for that any way. These photos make it look like every day was D-Day—and it sure felt like it at Fort Pierce.

1821—Marines Swarm Ashore.   Greetings from Fort Pierce, Florida.

1823—Beach Scene on "D" Day   Greetings from Fort Pierce, Florida.

27

1824—Loading Assault Boats. Greetings from Fort Pierce, Florida

1822—Sea Legs Drill at Fort Pierce, Florida.

names like Spanish Bayonet and Adam's Needles. They have thorns that are as sharp as they could be. And then there were the swamps, crawling through mud with snakes, and always mosquitos and sand fleas. Going in the water was no relief; the surf was thick with jelly fish. The sting of a man-o-war can make you long for a swarm of mosquitos.

We all went through a period of continuous night and day non-stop swimming, boating, running, swamp patrols, mock attacks on objectives, and setting off explosives that lasted some seven or eight days. This training was accomplished with almost no sleep and little food, which the men referred to as "the week from hell." It was designed to test us physically, mentally, and emotionally; to separate and weed out those who did not display the endurance, ability, and discipline to obey orders and complete missions under extreme stress and environmental conditions. It *was* pretty much like hell.

I survived the "Hell Week." I was in pretty good shape when I came into the Navy, and much of the physical part of the training seemed routine to me. In fact, I looked forward to the non-stop, grueling days of training, so you could say I was also mentally prepared.

Training for those of us surviving volunteers began to normalize into something of a routine after that week. The jetty and the ocean were omnipresent. Everywhere we went, the rubber boat was still with us. At first we thought this boat drill was intended to get us to quit the NCDU training program, but we soon recognized that it taught us togetherness and teamwork. Each man had to pull his weight—as a team. The more we pulled together, the easier the training seemed to become.

At this point, our demolition training became more intense. We learned how to blow up various types of obstacles and things that might be on the beaches where the landing craft of an invasion would go in.

This training later became known officially as "Hell Week," and it remains a key component and pervasive aspect of SEAL training and selection today. Hell Week was derived from the Scout and Raider School, where LCDR Draper Kauffman, the Officer in Charge of the NCDU School, asked the U.S. Army instructors if they could condense their month-long training program into one week.

Finally, this was what I had gone down there for! We used rubber hose stuffed with explosives. Each one was five feet in length with two pounds of TNT per foot. Funny the details you remember. We hauled stacks of those things around, which made all those hours of log-throwing pay off.

Training included quite a bit of improvisation. We were inventing how to do things more than we were learning established methods. We "boys" who were left to LCDR Kaufmann were a pretty creative and daring group. The Seabees were responsible for building the obstacles, and we were responsible for destroying them. You could say we had a bit of competition with those Seabees as they tried to think up designs they thought we could not destroy. It was hopeless for them. We destroyed everything and fast.

Training included recon skills too. We learned how to chart sandbars and reefs, how to find channels through them, or, when that wasn't possible, where to place the TNT to clear paths for ships.

Surf passage and casting takes constant practice and sure teamwork.

We are towing a rubber boat stacked with 20 pound haversacks of explosives.

A rare moment of rest with our beached rubber boats. The mosquitos were too small to show up in the picture, but they were there in force.

On top of conditioning, explosives training, and reconnoitering, we learned stealth. One evolution consisted of paddling our rubber boats; sometimes as many as five miles out into the ocean, before turning back. We would paddle to a "target" beach, hide our rubber boats, and infiltrate to objectives selected by our instructors. "Enemy" sentries were posted where we least expected them. If they caught us, they forced us to sit in place until the exercise was over, all the while enduring the sand fleas and mosquitoes eating away at every part of our exposed flesh.

If we successfully evaded the "enemy," we would patrol back to retrieve our hidden boats, paddle to the base camp for several hours of sleep, and then do the same thing all over again. In some training events, the "target" was a bag of Hershey® chocolate bars. Hershey bars remain the taste of success to me to this day.

We trained endlessly, but we still had time for a night on the town every now and then. There wasn't much town, mind you, but we did our best to enjoy it. There was just one place, as I recall, where you could buy a beer and dance with a girl.

In September 1943, the first NCDU class graduated. We were focused on getting ready to go fight and win a war. If you had told me back then that Class 1 was starting a legacy, I would not have believed you. At the time of this writing, men are going through training much like we went through as part of Class 300 and something.

By the time Class 1 graduated, we were down to ten five-man teams. Fewer than 50% of us had lasted through the almost three-months of training.

A close friend in training was Robert Bass. Here we are in front of a large barrel used for washing up at camp.

30

Back row: Harrison Q. Eskridge, Dillard E. Williams, and Sam Pahdopony.
Front row: James D. Sandy, Johnny N. Wilhide, and William L. Dawson.

We didn't have best friends on the teams. We trained together and lived together so closely, we were pretty much all each other's best friends. I can tell you that Sam Pahdopony was a very good man to have next to you in a very bad situation.

GOLDER - FLEMING - McDERMOTT - HARRING - DUNCAN

DIED IN THE INVASION OF NORMANDY 1944 JUNE

YETTER   KAUFFMAN

The men from our class who were sent to Normandy had an awful tough time. Entire boat crews were killed in the invasion. The NCDUs in France had a 53% casualty rate.

STONE – SOLTIS – ROLLINS – SMITH – TOMLINSON

SHINNER   KAUFFMAN

Robert Bass, Bill Armstrong, and another friend I can't identify.

Here is a picture of me in the tent city we called home in Fort Pierce.

NCDU-1, with Lieutenant Junior Grade Edwin Williams as Officer in Charge, left Fort Pierce before training was actually completed and deployed to aid the assault on Kiska in the Aleutian Islands of Alaska. Bill's unit, NCDU-2, along with NCDU-3, left Fort Pierce as soon as training was completed, and were not around for official graduation pictures.

Me with Alar Pierce.

Me with Johnny Wilhide.

At liberty in front of our house in Washington just before I left for the Pacific.

My friend Robert Bass was assigned to one of the units sent to Normandy.

I was in the best shape I had ever been in my life. I felt like I could whip the world. I just didn't know what part of the world I was going to go whip.

After training was completed, we were formed up into our permanent NCDU assignments. I was assigned to NCDU-2. The pressure was on the Navy brass to put us in the field right away. NCDU-1 was already deployed to Alaska. My unit, NCDU-2 and NCDU-3 got orders almost immediately.

Lawrence Connelly and I went to school together and ran around the neighborhood together. He joined the Army right around the time I joined the Navy.

A night on the town in Fort Pierce often included going to dances with girls in the town.

The remainder of Class 1 sat for formal individual and group graduation pictures. I have a good collection of photos that were sent to me by members of the class. There are no graduation portraits of NCDU-1 or NCDU-2. We were already gone by the time the photographers arrived.

I was given a few days to return to Washington, DC to say goodbye to my mother and father. I saw my close friends, Ed Nicholson, Lawrence Connelly and Cliff Henderson. We had grown up together and played football together. Now we were all going off to war, though not together. We all were going in different directions—and in a hurry.

Lawrence Connelly was a close friend of mine growing up in Washington, DC. His nickname was "Sunshine."

Clifford Henderson, 18, aviation radioman second class, is missing in action in the South Pacific, his parents, Mr. and Mrs. Philip O. Henderson, 4724 Third place N.W., have been notified.

Mrs. Henderson said she was not informed of the date her son disappeared. She only knew that he was on a dive-bomber. His last letter was dated April 11. A War Bond he had purchased with an allotment of pay arrived yesterday. He has purchased $1400 in War Bonds since he joined the Navy in July, 1942, his mother said.

Mr. Henderson.

He was born in Washington and attended Eliot Junior and Eastern High Schools. He was one of the outstanding players on the "Irish Aces," a sandlot football team. All 47 of the boys who used to play football in the neighborhood are now in the service, according to R. C. Roberts, District Fire Marshal and ardent supporter of athletics. *Wash-Star - May-14*

Lawrence Connelly.

Ed Nicholson (who was killed in the war), and another friend I used to play ball with, stopped by before we all went off for basic training.

Pfc. Grisso
(Liberated)

Pfc. Paul B. Grisso, jr., son of Paul B. Grisso, 238 Tenth street N.E., a Fire Department member for 23 years, has returned home after being liberated by the American 3d Army from a German hospital near Dresden.

A member of Company G, 422d Infantry, 106th Division of the 1st Army, Pfc. Grisso went overseas last October and was captured December 21 in the Ardennes breakthrough. He was taken first to Stalag 4-B, near Reisa, Germany, and later put to work under German civilian guards in a steel mill nearby. Still later he was transferred to railroad work near Dresden.

During his captivity, Pfc. Grisso said, the Germans allowed American prisoners only two and one-half slices of bread and a bowl of thin soup daily. Even this, he said, was withdrawn if the guards thought a prisoner's work was unsatisfactory.

Pfc. Grisso said he had been struck in the chest by a rifle butt wielded by a guard who was dissatisfied with his work in the steel mill and that political prisoners in the same mill were frequently lashed with "bull whips."

Because of his deficient diet and constant hard labor, Pfc. Grisso collapsed while working on a German railroad and was taken to a hospital, where elements of the 3d Army found him.

At the time of his capture, Pfc. Grisso said, he weighed 165 pounds, but during his captivity lost 59 pounds. Under the Army's care, which he praised highly, he has more than regained his weight, which is now 170. Pfc. Grisso is on leave until July 23, after which he expects he probably will be sent to the Pacific.

Pfc. Edwin V. Nicholson

Reburial services for Pfc. Edwin Vernon Nicholson, U.S.M.C.R., son of Shelton and Zanis Nicholson, 1629 A St. NW., will be held at 2 p.m. today in Arlington National cemetery.

Pfc. Nicholson was killed in action on Okinawa on June 16, 1945, while serving with the 5th Marines, 1st Marine division.

A native Washingtonian, he was a student at Eastern high school when he enlisted in the Marine Corps. He played football at Eastern and was chosen a member of the all-high team.

Pfc. Nicholson also was an active member of the Washington Boys club and Epworth Methodist church.

In addition to his parents, he is survived by four sisters, Mrs. Nellie Nichols, Mrs. Bernice Spigone, Mrs. Evelyn Johnson, and Mary white, and a brother, Floyd S. Nicholson, all of Washington.

Pfc. Nicholson

★ Bass, Robert W., GM2c, USNR, Durham, N. C.: As a member of a naval combat demolition unit in the 7th Beach Battalion during the Normandy invasion, he fearlessly proceeded in the face of heavy German artillery, machinegun and rifle fire and worked tirelessly with his crew to clear a section of the beach. Although seven of the 12-man unit were killed

or wounded, they succeeded in blasting a 50-yard gap through the treacherous and formidable beach obstacles. After completing the mission, Bass again braved the enemy barrage to render aid to his men and was himself wounded while carrying injured crewmates to safety. He contributed materially to the success of the Allied offensive in that area.

Robert W. Bass
GM2c, USNR

My friend Robert Bass was in the NCDU on OMAHA beach that received one of only three Presidential Unit Citations awarded to the Navy for the Normandy landings. He earned the Navy Cross that day for heroism; as did several others from the unit.

Missing *Buzzy*

Lt. (j. g.) Charles E. Weickhardt, jr., 23, U. S. N. R., son of Lt. Comdr. and Mrs. Weickhardt, 1239 Forty-fifth place S.E., was reported missing March 29 in the Pacific area. Lt. Weickhardt was a fighter pilot attached to an aircraft carrier. He entered active duty in January, 1940, after having entered the naval reserve at the age of 17, his mother said.

A native of the District, he was graduated from Eastern High School and had attended George Washington University before going overseas in November, 1943. He spent 14 months overseas, his mother said, and had been awarded the Air Medal. He had been recommended for the gold star in lieu of a second Air Medal, his mother said. A brother, Dr. George D. Weickhardt, is attached to St. Elizabeth's Hospital.

Stories about the following, listed on today's official casualty list as missing, previously appeared in The Star when next of kin were notified.
Edward G. Curtin, aviation radio-

Posthumous Honors Awarded 2 Navy Men

The navy has presented an Air Medal to Philip Oliver Henderson, of Washington, for his son, the late Clifford Oliver Henderson, aviation radioman second class, U.S.N. The medal was awarded for "meritorious achievement in aerial flight" as air crewman in bombing squadron 2, attached to the carrier Hornet, operating against the Japs, in March 1944. The award and citation were presented by Rear Adm. Glenn B. Davis, commandant, Potomac River Naval Command. Another posthumous award, the Distinguished Flying Cross, was presented Alfred Babineau, of Washington, for his son, Leo Joseph Edward, AMMF second class, for "extraordinary service during the war."

Chapter 3
Going to War

After training, things started happening pretty fast. Three units went to Europe. My unit was NCDU-2 and, together with NCDU-3, we boarded a train headed west—bound for the Pacific Theatre.

We processed through Treasure Island in the San Francisco Bay, and were granted two weeks of leave for exploring the area. We had a great time in San Francisco. The whole town was very supportive, and there seemed to be some sort of dance or event at a club every night. It was a good time to be a man in a uniform. The war, for me, at this point, was a good time.

Johnny Wilhide.

I had one last photo taken of me to send home.

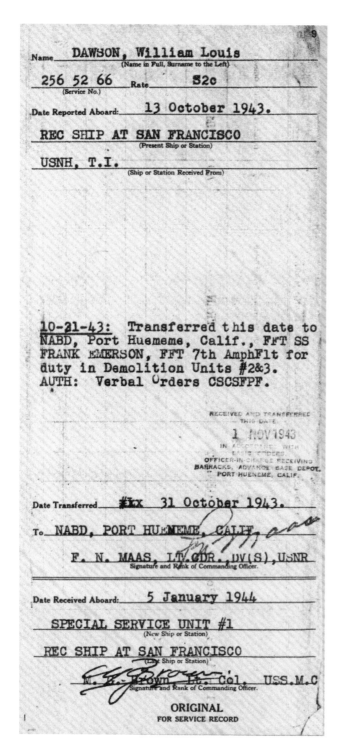

"Do sailors make good husbands?"
"I don't know, they sometimes
make bad wives."

I enjoyed collecting humorous postcards to send home and send to friends. I kept quite a few for myself.

Falling Barometer

A bugler, sad, 2 rel8, Came aboard in a terrible st8; Though he drank 5 glasses of whiskey str8, He st6 2 the story 'twas something he 8!

COPR. 1943 EX. SUP. CO., CHGO.,   MADE IN U.S.A.

Combat Forces

"Well, Commander, I think the patient is well enough to report for duty!"

COPR. 1943 EX. SUP. CO., CHGO., MADE IN U.S.A.

Starboard Watch

"Oh Captain!
I forgot to close your bathroom last night—
lookit what's here!

COPR. 1943 EX. SUP. CO., CHGO., MADE IN U.S.A.

Every Man for Himself

"That's what I get for believing everything I hear
—five ports so far and not a single sweetheart."

COPR. 1943 EX. SUP. CO., CHGO., MADE IN U.S.A.

Three Point Landing

"I think the wind direction is just right Commander!"

COPR. 1943 EX. SUP. CO., CHGO., MADE IN U.S.A.

"This is the third time this week the S.Ps have raided the Red Hot and Blue Club."

COPR. 1943 EX. SUP. CO., CHGO.,   MADE IN U.S.A.

Haircut, Ma'am?

COPR. 1943 EX. SUP. CO., CHGO.,   MADE IN U.S.A.

"Can't you forget for tonight that you're in the navy?"

COPR. 1943 EX. SUP. CO., CHGO.,   MADE IN U.S.A.

Speed and secrecy combined to create confusion that would follow us across the Pacific and into battle. Lieutenant Junior Grade Frank Kaine was the officer in charge of NCDU-2, and also was the most senior officer of all the NCDUs in the Pacific. He turned out to be able to quickly move things along, even if he didn't actually sort things out. That was fine with all of us. Sometimes it was much to our benefit to keep some people confused some of the time. From the minute we stepped foot on the base in Fort Pierce, we knew we were different and that the Navy's rules didn't quite apply to us as much as they applied to everyone else.

Some years after the war, I was able to get a copy of a letter written by a low-level officer expressing some frustration surrounding the confusion about who we were, where we were going, and even what our unit numbers were.

Dear Mr. Kauffman:

We urgently need your cooperation on clearing up a matter which is causing consideration trouble in the movement of the first eleven demolition units.

I just talked with someone on the staff of ComServPacSuborComd from San Francisco, and the poor fellow was completely mystified by the conflict between the numbers of the units given by you when you ordered them out and the destinations to which the units were assigned. For example, he said he had an Ensign Hawkes who claimed to be Unit No. 1, which made him supernumerary. Also, an Ensign Kaine (so it sounded over the phone) who claimed to be Unit No. 10, which made him also supernumerary on the West Coast. He was asking our permission to juggle the Units as best he could so as to get two Units for SeventhPhib, two for ThirdPhib, and three for FifthPhib as required.

I told him to disregard completely the Unit numbers contained in the Officers' orders, or claimed verbally by the officers them-selves, and to assign the Units as follows:

<u>WEST COAST UNITS</u>

Unit No. 2	– Kaine to EDUR	– SoWesPac
3	– Anderson to EDUR	– SoWesPac
4	– Morris to EPIC	– SoPac
5	– Cartee to EPIC	– SoPac
6	– Gordon to IRON	– Central Pacific
7	– King to IRON	– Central Pacific
8	– Hawkes to IRON	– Central Pacific

I am carrying the thing completely through by specifying the Numbers for Allen, Jacobs and Heideman.

<u>EAST COAST UNITS</u>

Unit No. 9	– Allen	– Mediterranean
10	– Jacobs	– Mediterranean
11	– Heidman	– Europe

Will you, Sir, get C.O., ATB, Fort Pierce, to issue a modification of each of the above officer's orders so as to specify that his Unit's number will read in accordance with the schedule shown on the above page. Unless this done, and done fairly soon, absolutely none of your men will ever get their mail; to say nothing of how many more times they will run into trouble enroute as to whether or not they are where they belong to be.

If any of the enlisted men's orders contain any reference whatsoever to the Number of the Unit to which they are assigned, then their orders should likewise be modified to conform with the schedule shown on page one of this letter.

I am sending copies of this letter to all of the officers mentioned above in order that they may start telling their people how to address their mail properly.

Respectfully,

JOHN McNEILL SMITH, JR.
Lieut.(jg) USNR

Lt. Comdr. D. L. Kauffman
    Naval Combat Demolition Units Project
        Amphibious Training Base
            Fort Pierce, Florida

-2-

The ladies in San Francisco liked me pretty well, and I liked them too.

William Armstrong in camp.

Me outside our barracks.

Back row: Cornelius C. De Vries, William J. Armstrong, Edward A. Messall, and Dillard E. Williams. Front row: Alar H. Pierce, me, and Johnny Wilhide.

The fun in San Francisco did not last. We were ordered to Port Hueneme, California, a bit north of Los Angeles. Waiting there for us was the liberty ship *Frank C. Emerson*. We boarded along with 200 tons of high explosives and began our slow journey to Australia on November 3, 1943.

Port Hueneme was a base for the west coast Mobile Construction Battalions or Seabee's. Liberty ships were standardized 10,000-ton cargo ships designed for quick construction in large numbers during World War II. They were the product of the industrialist Henry J. Kaiser, who got into mass-production shipbuilding as a part of the war effort.

Liberty ships don't travel very fast—especially when trying to avoid submarine attacks. Still, we were in high spirits when we crossed the equator. New sailors, called pollywogs, got initiated during a ceremony honoring King Neptune. Some guys shaved their heads to celebrate. It was all in fun and it helped break the monotony.

To while away the hours crossing the Pacific, I created an insignia for our unit. Our shipmates called us powder monkeys, so I created a character with the dynamite in his tail. I put that character on the cover of my log book in which I started recording significant dates on the crossing to Australia.

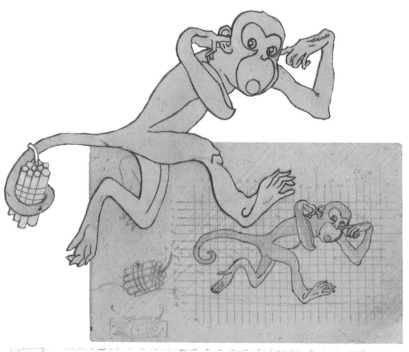

Some men shaved their heads when we crossed the equator. I personally refused to do it. I wanted to keep my hair.

46

Intelligence planners knew that the Japanese never used mines or barricades as profusely or as cleverly as the Germans, but it was not known in what manner, with what obstacles, or to what extent the enemy might employ such devices to prevent or impede future landings.

On 19 November 1943, over 5,000 U.S. Marines invaded at Tarawa in the Gilbert Islands. Within a few days, over half of them were dead. Many of those who died were killed on the coral reef approach to Tarawa's beaches. The landing craft had lodged on the reef, not Japanese obstacles, leaving the Marines helpless in a withering Japanese crossfire. Vice Admiral Richmond Kelly Turner, Commander of the U. S. Pacific Amphibious Fleet, vowed that this would never happen again.

As 1944 approached, U.S. forces had nearly conquered the vast Solomon Island area. United States Army and Australian forces, under the command of General Douglas MacArthur, were beginning to pound the Japanese at New Guinea, and the U.S. military was preparing its long march across the western Pacific toward Japan. With Tarawa and the remainder of the Gilbert Islands behind them, the next objective was the Japanese-occupied Marshall Islands with three fortified Japanese strongholds: Kwajalein, Roi-Namur, and Eniwetok. It was into this situation that Bill Dawson and his teammates arrived.

Chapter 4
My War Log Book

I wasn't supposed to keep a diary, so I guess you could say I broke the rules a little bit with my log book. The Navy never put anything in our records about what we did either, because it was all top secret. I kept my log entries limited to some very few basics, and only wrote entries well after our operations were complete. Operations that were classified I didn't include at all.

We took secrecy very seriously back then. We didn't talk to anyone about what we did, when, where, or how we did it. I still won't talk about some of the things. I don't understand the men today who feel the need to rush out and write tell-all books and do television specials. The rest of my team are gone. I am the only one left to tell the tales. I would never let my teammates down or spoil the honor they so richly deserve by spilling the beans now or trying to shine the spotlight only on me. My story is a story about our unit, not an individual.

Even 70 years after the events, I still won't talk about the details of our operations. The ocean currents of the South China Sea haven't changed all that much in the decades since the war. The techniques we innovated in 1943 are still used by the SEAL teams today. To provide the public with specifics would blunt the effectiveness of what we do and put today's heroes in danger. There isn't any amount of money or fame in the world that would make me willing to jump in front of a television camera or to write about the details of what we did back then.

NAVAL COMBAT DEMOLITION UNITS

#2

FRANK R. KAINE
2 BELMONT
BRATTLEBORO VT.

WILLIAM J. ARMSTRONG
RT. 2 BOX 16
BEAVERTON, OREGON

WILLIAM L. DAWSON
1801 B ST. S.E.
WASHINGTON, D.C.

ALAR H. PIERCE
2401 MOORE AVE.
ANNISTON, ALABAMA

DILLARD E. WILLIAMS
TAPOCO
NORTH, CAROLINA

JOHNY N. WILHIDE
BOX 248 SWANNANOA
NORTH, CAROLINA

#3

LLOYD
~~LOLLIE~~ G. ANDERSON
458½ W VERN
LOS ANGELES CALIF.

CORNELIUS C. DE VRIES
7810 5ᵀᴴ AVE. N.E.
SEATTLE WASHINGTON

HARRISON Q. ESKRIDGE
726 N. WASH. ST.
RUTHERFORDTON N.C.

EDWARD A. MESSALL
510 N. 2ⁿᵈ ST.
MARLOW OKLAHOMA

SAM PAHDOPONY
BOX 556
LAWTON OKLAHOMA

JAMES D. SANDY
1409 G ST. N.E.
WASHINGTON D.C.

APRIL, 14, 1943.
ENLISTED U.S.N.   WASHINGTON D.C.
APRIL 14 To JUNE 30
BAINBRIDGE MD. U.S.N.T.S.
JULY 2 To SEP 8   N.C.D.U. TRAINING
A.T.B. FORT PIERCE FLA.
SEP. 18 To OCT. 15
TREASURE ISLAND   SAN FRANCISCO CALIF.
OCT. 15 To OCT. 28
WENT HOME ON LEAVE
OOT. 28 To OCT. 31
TREASURE ISLAND
OCT. 31
WE LEFT FRISCO BY TRAIN FOR HUENEME
NOV. 3
LEFT HUENEME ON THE FRANK C. EMERSON
NOV. 13 1943
CROSSED EQUATOR 9:05 A.M.
NOV. 22
CROSSED INTERNATIONAL DATE LINE
NOV. 27
ARRIVED BRISBANE AUSTRALIA
DEC. 26
LEFT BRISBANE

GUINEA
Where the breezes blow like zephyrs thru the
tents across the bay,
Where the soldiers stand like sentinels as they
watch the fishes play,
Yes, there is no place like Guinea (thank God
for that, I say),
Who wants a place like Guinea,
When there is the good old U.S.A.
APO 704   —Cpl. MILTON KRON

DEC. 29
ARRIVED TOWNSVILLE   AUSTRALIA
DEC. 31
LEFT TOWNSVILLE,
JAN. 3 (1944)
ARRIVED MILNEY BAY NEW GUINEA
JAN 5
ARRIVED DAWA DAWA
MAR. 3
LEFT DAWA ON THE WESTRALIA FOR
BUNA, LEFT BUNA ON L.S.T. 466
*MAR. 9 (2)
ARRIVED ADMIRALTY ISLANDS
MAR. 23
LEFT ADMIRALTYS ON DESTROYER STEVENSON
MAR. 24
ARRIVED AT CAPE CRETIN 15MILES FROM FINCHAVEN
APRIL. 15
LEFT FOR AITAPE INV. ON L.S.T. 453
APRIL 17
ARRIVED AT ADMIRALTYS TRANSFERED TO Y.M.S. 51
*APRIL 22 - (2)
ARRIVED AT AITAPE, SAW PLENTY OF ACTION
APRIL 23
LEFT AITAPE ON L.S.T. 181 TO CAPE CRETIN

51

1944

MAY, 17
    LEFT CAPE CRETIN ON LCI. 448.
MAY, 20
    ARRIVED AT HOLLANDIA.
MAY, 25
    LEFT HOLLANDIA, STILL ON LCI. 448.
* MAY, 27 -(3)
    ARRIVED, BIAK, 2 AIR RAIDS, 5 JAP PLANES.
MAY, 28
    BIAK, 2 AIR RAIDS , 1 BILLY MITCHEL .
MAY, 29
    BIAK, 2 AIR RAIDS, 2 JAP PLANES, LCI. 448 GOT ONE.
MAY, 30,
    BIAK, 2 AIR RAIDS, 1 JAP PLANE, SHOT DOWN.
MAY, 31
    BIAK, 2 AIR RAIDS, 2 JAP PLANES SHOT DOWN.
JUNE, 1
    FINISHED BLASTING CHANEL, 2 AIR RAIDS,
    BOMBING AT NIGHT,
JUNE, 2
    THREE AIR RAIDS, 10 PLANES SHOT DOWN, "JAP,"
    LCI. 448 GOT ONE.
JUNE, 3
    2 AIR RAIDS, DIVE BOMBERS JEST MISED CAN
    ONE MAN KILLED.

1944

JUNE, 4
    JAP TASK FORCE HEAPED THIS WAY, BIAK,
    TWO AIR RAIDS, NIGHT BOMBING,
    OUR FORCE ARRIVED,
JUNE, 5
    2 AIR RAIDS, EARLY MORNING, BOMBING,
    LEFT BIAK, SHIP SLIGHTLY DAMAGED, -
JUNE, 6
    ARRIVED HOLLANDIA, STILL ON LCI. 448
JUNE, 11
    LEFT HOLLANDIA,
JUNE, 14
    ARRIVED CAPE CRETIN,
JUNE, 15
    LEFT CAPE CRETIN,
JUNE, 16
    ARRIVED MADANG, LEFT LCI. 448,
    WENT ABOARD LCI. 227,
JUNE, 25
    LEFT MADANG, ON LCI. 227.
JUNE, 27
    ARRIVED HOLLANDIA,
JUNE, 28
    LEFT HOLLANDIA,

1944

JUNE, 29
   ARRIVED WADKE, ISLAND.
JUNE, 30
   LEFT WADKE,
JULY, 1
   PAST BIAK, ISLAND
✱ JULY, 2 - (4)
   ARRIVED NOEMFOOR ISLAND, D-DAY.
JULY, 4
   WENT ASHORE, LOTS OF DEAD JAPS. AND
   PLANES. BOMBING AT NIGHT.
JULY, 7
   LEFT NOEMFOOR,
JULY, 10
   ARRIVED HOLLANDIA
JULY, 11
   LEFT HOLLANDIA,
JULY, 12
   ARRIVED MADANG,
JULY, 13
   LEFT MADANG,
JULY, 15
   ARRIVED CAPE CRETIN.
JULY, 15
   LEFT CAPE CRETIN.

ALLIED FORCES LAND UNDER COVER OF NAVAL AND AIR BOMBARDMENT

See 4 July.

ADVANCED ALLIED HEADQUARTERS ON NEW GUINEA—*Noemfoor Island:* Our ground forces have landed at Kamiri on Noemfoor Island, 100 statute miles west of our Biak Island airfields. The movement was an amphibious one, and the troops went ashore through the surf under cover of naval and air bombardment.

Landings were made through narrow and difficult coral reefs, generally regarded as impracticable for such a purpose. As a result the location of the attack was completely unexpected by the enemy and his defense preparations were outflanked.

Our forces consequently landed with practically no loss, either ground, naval or air units, and promptly secured the airfield, our main objective, without a struggle. Thirty partially damaged airplanes were captured by our ground troops on the field.

The seizure of this base will give added breadth and depth to our air deployment, and will further dislocate the enemy's South Seas defenses, already seriously shaken by our previous advances.

1944

JULY, 17
   ARRIVED MILNE BAY.
JULY, 18
   ARRIVED AT GAMADOTA.
JULY, 24
   LEFT GAMADOTA ON LURLINE,
JULY, 27
   ARRIVED BRISBANE.
AUG, 1
   LEFT BRISBANE BY PBM FOR
   SYDNEY AUSTRALIA,
AUG, 14
   LEFT SYDNEY BY TRAIN.
AUG, 15
   ARRIVED BRISBANE
AUG, 20
   WENT ABOARD SS. CHAS H. WINDHAM.
AUG, 21
   LEFT BRISBAINE,
AUG, 26
   ARRIVED GAMADOPO. MILNE BAY.
AUG, 28
   WENT ABOARD LC.I. 228,
SEPT. 16.
   STILL IN MILNE BAY, LOADED EXPLOSIVES,

1944

SEPT. 26.
LEFT MILNE BAY ON LCI 228 LOADED WITH
ABOUT 40 TONS OF EXPLOSIVES.

SEPT. 28.
01:53 GOT RAMMED BY L.C.I. 340.

SEPT. 29.
ARRIVED HOLLANDIA.

SEPT. 30.
UNLOADED ALL THE EXPLOSIVES ONTO L.C.T.

OCT. 9.
SAW UNIT 24 FOR THE FIRST TIME IN OVER A
YEAR. THEY WERE IN THE NORMANDY LANDING.

OCT. 13
LEFT HOLLANDIA AT 13:00 136 SHIPS IN THE
CONVOY.

OCT. 14.
CROSSED EQUATOR.

*OCT. 20 - (5) MADE RECONNAISSANCE OF BEACH
ARRIVED IN SAN PEDRO BAY AT DAWN. LANDING WAS
MADE ON LEYTE. L.C.I. 71 & 72 HIT FROM BEACH, PHILIPPINES.

OCT. 24.
ONE AIR RAID AFTER ANOTHER, (L.C.I. 1065 SUNK.)
(L.C.I. 65 CRASHED BY PLANE) (TUG SUNK.) 29 JAP PLANES
SHOT DOWN. THINK WE GOT ONE.

1944

OCT. 26.
AIR RAIDS ALL DAY. BOMBING AND STRAFING. BIG
NAVAL BATTLE.

OCT. 27.
SEVEN AIR RAIDS. LIBERTY HIT BY CRASHDIVE.
TOTAL JAP PLANES TO DATE 200.

OCT. 29.
THREE AIR RAIDS AT DAWN. A TYPHOON STARTED
AT 23:30

OCT. 30.
WHAT A NIGHT. TYPHOON EASED OFF AT 05:00.

NOV. 3.
AIR RAIDS ALL NIGHT LONG. 10 PLANES SHOT DOWN.

NOV. 4.
AIR RAID IN MORNING. A P.T. HIT.

NOV. 8
TYPHOON STARTED 12:00.

NOV. 9.
TYPHOON QUIT 08:00 WE WERE NEARLY ON THE BEACH.

NOV. 12.
THREE AIR RAIDS 7 SHIPS HIT, 4 LIBERTYS, 2 L.C.I.
ONE L.S.T. 12 JAPS SHOT DOWN.

NOV. 14.
THREE AIR RAIDS, 9 JAPS SHOT DOWN.
BLASTED P.B.Y.

1944

NOV. 16.

 HAVE BEEN BLASTING THE LAST FEW DAYS
FOR P.B.Y. SLIP. 9 JAPS SHOT DOWN THE 14TH.

NOV. 19.

 WENT TO TACKLOBAN, VERY DIRTY PLACE, GOT
SOME MONEY ORDERS AN SOME PHILIPPINE MONEY.

NOV. 23.

 QUIET ALL DAY, AIR RAID AT DUSK, LIBERTY HIT.
WENT TO TACKLOBAN THAT AFTERNOON.

NOV. 24.

 AIR RAID ON AIR STRIP 6 RAIDS ALTOGATHER.
22 JAP PLANES SHOT DOWN.

NOV. 27.

 TWO AIR RAIDS DURING DAY. CAN HIT IN DRYDOCK.
CRASH DIVE. RAIDS AT NIGHT. 15 JAPS SHOT DOWN.

DEC. 7

 15 JAPS SHOT DOWN.

DEC. 12.

 LEFT TACKLOBAN AT 13:30. ON L.C.I. 228.

DEC. 13.

 GOING THROUGH MINDANAO SEA, AIR RAID STARTED
AT 15:00 CRUISER NASHVILL WAS CRASH DIVED.
ABOUT 125 MEN KILLED.

DEC. 14.

 AT SEA. SOME A.A. FIRE BUT DID NOT SEE
ANY PLANES.

1944

* DEC. 15 - (6)
JAP SHIP SUNK BY CANS AT 05:00 AIR
RAIDS SOON AFTER. BOMBARDMENT OF
MINDORO STARTED AT 07:00. TROOPS LANDED
AT 07:30. EIGHT JAP PLANES CAME IN AT
08:25 ALL DOWNED. THREE CRASHED INTO
TWO L.S.T. WE GOT HITS ON ONE. LEFT
MINDORO AT 10:00.

DEC. 17.
AT SEA. ONE PLANE RAID. WAS SHOT DOWN.

DEC. 18.
ARRIVED AT TACKLOBAN AT 10:30

DEC. 20.
AIR RAID AT DUSK. NO DAMAGE DONE. ONE
JAP PLANE SHOT DOWN.

DEC. 22.
UNLOADED ALL OUR T.N.T. ON A.K. 95.

DEC. 23.
WENT TO TACKLOBAN. NOTHING THERE.
GOT A PUNCHING BAG FROM THE ARMY.

DEC. 24.
WENT TO TACKLOBAN ON MAIL RUN. GOT
THREE LETTERS FOR XMAS. HAD A FEW
CANS OF BEER. AIR RAID. ONE PLANE
SHOT DOWN,

1944

DEC. 25.
QUIET ALL DAY. AIR RAIDS ALL NIGHT.

JAN. 2, (1945)
WENT ABOARD THE CLEMPSON, (A.P.D. #31)
LEFT LEYTE AT 2300.

JAN. 4.
TWO AIR RAIDS IN EARLY A.M. QUIET ALL DAY.
ANOTHER AIR RAID AT 1720. THE OMMNEY
BAY WAS LOST. (C.V.E.)

JAN. 5.
AIR RAID IN MORNING. THEY TRIED TO
CRASHDIVE THE C.V.E. BUT MISSED. ANOTHER
RAID AT 1620. WE GOT 3 JAPS AT THE SAME
TIME. ONE C.V.E. HIT. LOUVILLE HIT. AUSSIE-
DD HIT. COLUMBIA HIT. SHARPSHIRE HIT.

* JAN. 6. - (7)
ARRIVED OFF THE WEST COAST OF LUZON.
STARTED TO SHELL THE BEACH. ALSO SANK
TWO JAP TANKERS NEAR THE BEACH.
SHELLING STARTED AT 1115. DD SUMMNER
HIT. DD WALKE HIT. APD. BROOKS HIT.
BB NEW MEX. HIT. CL. AUSTRALIA HIT TWO TIMES.
WENT INSIDE LINGAYAN GOLF. AND SHELLED
A LITTLE.

1945

JAN. 7.

AIR RAID AT 0415. D.M.S. HIT A MINE AND SUNK. AT 1445 STARTED TO SHELL THE BEACH. TO COVER DEMO. PARTY. SECURED AT 1700. AIR RAID AT 1845. D.M.S. #5 HIT AND SUNK. THE BROOKS SUNK.

JAN. 8.

AIR RAID AT 0720. SHELLED THE BEACH ALL DAY.

JAN. 9.

AIR RAIDS STARTED BEFORE DAWN. STILL SHELLING THE BEACH. THE TROOPS LANDED ABOUT 0930. ON LUZON. MORE AIR RAIDS STARTED AT 1305. BB MISSISSIPPI HIT. C.L. AUST. HIT AND LOST ONE STACK.

JAN. 10.

L.S.T. SUNK BY TORPEDO AT 0420. AN APA., L.C.I. AND DD DAMAGED BY JAP DEMO. AIR RAID AT 1910. DE HIT. APA. HIT.

JAN. 11.

WE WERE RAMMED BY P.A. 152 AT 0800. AIR RAID AT 1855.

JAN. 12.

SEVERAL AIR RAIDS IN THE MORNING. APD. #34, D.E. AND TWO MERCHANTMEN HIT.

JAN. 13.

REPAIRS ON SHIP COMPLEATED AND WE SHOVED OFF AT 1730.

JAN. 18.

ARRIVED IN LEYTE GULF AT 0700.

JAN. 19.

LEFT THE A.P.D. AND WENT BACK ON L.C.I. 228.

JAN. 21.

WENT ASHORE FOR A WHILE IN TACKLOBAN.

JAN. 24.

WENT IN DRYDOCK AT 1530.

JAN. 26.

LEFT DRYDOCK AT 0830.

FEB. 2.

WENT ASHORE IN TACKLOBAN ON MAIL RUN.

FEB. 3.

WENT ASHORE ON LIBERTY ON SAMAR.

FEB. 8.

LOADED T.N.T. SHOVED OFF AT 1700.

FEB. 10.

AT SEA. PRETTY ROUGH.

FEB. 11.

AT SEA. AND ROUGH. LEFT CONVOY AT 1800 TO ESCORT 227.

1945

FEB. 12.
SIGHTED LUZON IN EARLY MORNING.
STILL ROUGH. HEADING FOR SUBIC BAY.
ENTERED SUBIC BAY AT 1800.

FEB. 13.
STANDING BY FOR ORDERS. SHOULD LEAVE
TONIGHT ON P.T. TRIP TO MANILA BAY. CANCELED

FEB. 21.
FUELED UP.

FEB. 22.
WENT ASHORE ON GRANDIE ISLAND.

MARCH 1.
TOOK ON WATER AND WENT ASHORE
TO LOOK AROUND.

MARCH. 4.
LOADED STORES. SHOVED OFF AT 1030
FOR MINDORO.

MARCH. 5.
ARRIVED AT MINDORO AT 0800.

MARCH. 7.
THE CAPTAIN WENT HOME, KEARNS
TOOK OVER.

MARCH. 8.
SHOVED OFF AT 0730 FOR ZAMBOANGA.
ROUGH SEA.

1945

★ MARCH 10. - (8)
ARRIVED OFF ZAMBOANGA IN EARLY
MORNING G.Q. AT 0645. BOMBARDMENT
STARTED SOON AFTER. TROOPS LANDED AT
0915. PUT TO SEA AT 1830.

MAR. 11.
PUT IN AT ZAMBOANGA AT 0800 AFTER
A VERY ROUGH NIGHT AT SEA. QUIET ALL
DAY. PUT TO SEA AGAIN AT 1745.

MAR. 12.
PUT IN AT ZAMBOANGA AGAIN AT 0730.
ANOTHER ROUGH NIGHT. LOOKED FOR
MINES ALONG SHORE AND DOCK AREAS
ALL AFTERNOON. PICKET DUTY ALL NIGHT.

MAR. 13.
TOOK ON WATER. SHOVED OFF AT 1800
FOR LEYTE. AIR RAID AT 1812. NO DAMAGE.
SEA VERY ROUGH.

MAR. 15.
ARRIVED AT LEYTE AT 1730.

MAR. 22.
SHOVED OFF AT 13:30. ARRIVED AT
HANUNANGAN BAY AT 2100.

MAR. 24.
PUT TO SEA AT 1800 FOR CEBU.

1945

★ MAR. 26. - (9)
ARRIVED OFF CEBU AT DAWN,
BOMBARDMENT STARTED AT 0700,
TROOPS HIT BEACH AT 0830,
WE CLEARED BEACH OBSTICALS
ALL MORNING, BEACH WAS ALL MINED.

MAR. 27.
AIR RAID AT 1935, SOUNDED G.Q.
BY FIREING.

MAR. 29.
BLASTED IN THE HARBOR.

MAR. 30.
MORE BLASTING.

APRIL 1.
LOOKED OVER THE CITY OF
CEBU, IT'S ALL TORN TO HELL,
THE PEOPLE NEARLY STARVED.

APRIL 3.
DIVING FOR JAP SUB. NO LUCK.

APRIL 4.
LEFT CEBO AT 0745 FOR LEYTE.

APRIL 5.
ARRIVED OFF DULOG, LEYTE AT
1600, RECEIVED A LITTLE MAIL.

1945

APRIL 8.
SHOVED OFF FOR MINDORO AT
0600. ANTI-AIR-CRAFT TARGET
PRACTICE WHILE UNDER WAY.

APRIL 9.
ARRIVED AT MINDORO AT 1400.
RECEIVED MORE BACK MAIL.

APRIL 11.
SHOVED OFF FOR MANOUVERS AT
0630. RETURNED AT 1330.

APRIL 14.
LEFT MINDORO AT 1100.

APRIL 16.
PASSED BY ZAMBOANGA.

★ APRIL 17 - (10)
ARRIVED IN POLLOCK HARBOR
AT DAWN. BOMBARMENT OF BEACH
WAS LIGHT. TROOPS LANDED AT 0900,

APRIL 18.
QUITE ALL DAY, ANOTHER YEAR
FOR FATHER ; TIME.

APRIL 23.
LEFT POLLOCK HARBOR AT 1700
FOR ZAMBOANGA. MINDANAO.

60

1945

APRIL, 24.
ARRIVED AT ZAMBOANGA AT
0800. GOT ALL THE BANNANERS
AND PINEAPPLES WE WANTED.

APRIL. 25.
LEFT ZAMBOANGA FOR TARAKAN.
BORNEO,

APRIL. 26.
WENT TO G.Q. AT 0900. JAPS ON
RAFT'S OFF OF   ISLAND. WE
INVESTIGATED. GOT FIVE JAPS.
PLANES GOT ABOUT SIX RAFTS, LCI.
GOT TWO RAFTS. HELD CONFERENCE,
ARE TO GO IN 0-1. CLEAR OUT ALL
OBSTACLES.

★ APRIL. 27. - (11)
ARRIVED OFF TARARAN AND ANCHORED,
SWEEPER'S IN, TASK FORCE LAYED OFF.
UNDERWAY AT DUSK.

APRIL 28.
RETURNED TO SAME PLACE, ANCHORED.
YMS HIT MINE. LEFT AT DUSK,

APRIL, 29.
LCS. & Y.M.S. DREW FIRE FROM BEACH.

1945

APRIL 30.
ARRIVED AT TARAKAN, BOMBARTMENT.
AUSSIE DEMO. WENT IN AT 1100
UNDER SMOKE SCREEN,

MAY, 1. - .
BOMBARMENT OF BEACH, TROOPS
LANDED AT 0730. WE WENT IN
ABOUT 0900 TO HELP AUSSIE DEMO.
CLEAR OBSTACLES, SNIPER FIRE. LEFT
LCV. HIGH & DRY ON BEACH. OLLSO
L.S.T. WERE LEFT HIGH.

MAY, 2.
WENT IN TO BEACH AGAIN. NO WORK.
SNIPER FIRE,

MAY, 5.
LEFT TARAKAN, BORNO. FOR MOROTAI,

MAY, 8.
ARRIVED AT MOROTAI. AT 1700.

JUNE, 4.
LEFT MOROTAI FOR BORNEO,
HIT SOMETHING IN WATER BENT SHAFT.
WENT BACK TO MOROTAI FOR REPAIRED.
TWO MEN FELL OVER BOARD ON THE
WAY BACK, I WENT IN TO HELP, SAVED BOTH

JUNE, 5.
    LEFT MOROTAI ON L.C.I. 577 FOR
    BRUNEI BAY, BORNEO.
★ JUNE 11. (12)
    ARRIVED AT BRUNEI BAY. BORNEO, LEFT
    L.C.I. 577 WENT ABOARD A.P.D. 120.
    (JUNE) LEFT BRUNI FOR MOROTAI.
JUNE, 14,
    ARRIVED AT MOROTAI, LEFT A.P.D.
    WENT ABOARD L.C.I. 228.
JUNE, 15.
    LEFT L.C.I. 228. BOARDED L.C.I. 687.
    FOR TRANSPORTATION TO LEYTE.
JUNE. 19.
    ARRIVED LEYTE.
JUNE. 20.
    LEFT L.C.I. 687. WENT TO RECEIVING
    STATION ON SAMAR NAVY 3964.
JULY. 2.
    LEFT NAVY 3964 AND WENT ABOARD
    A.P.A. 199. U.S.S. MAGOFFIN.
JULY, 3.
    LEFT LEYTE ON P.A. 199 HEADED
    FOR HONOLULU.

JULY 15.
    ARRIVED IN HONOLULU

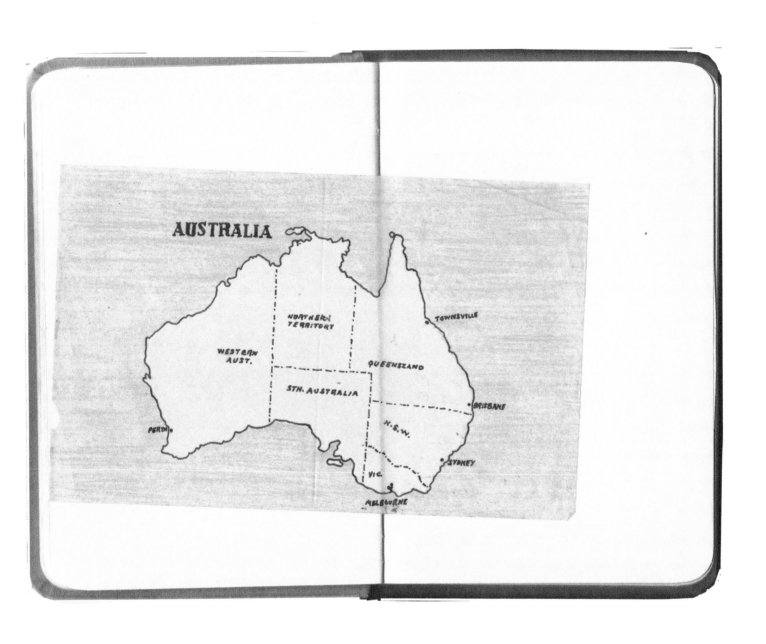

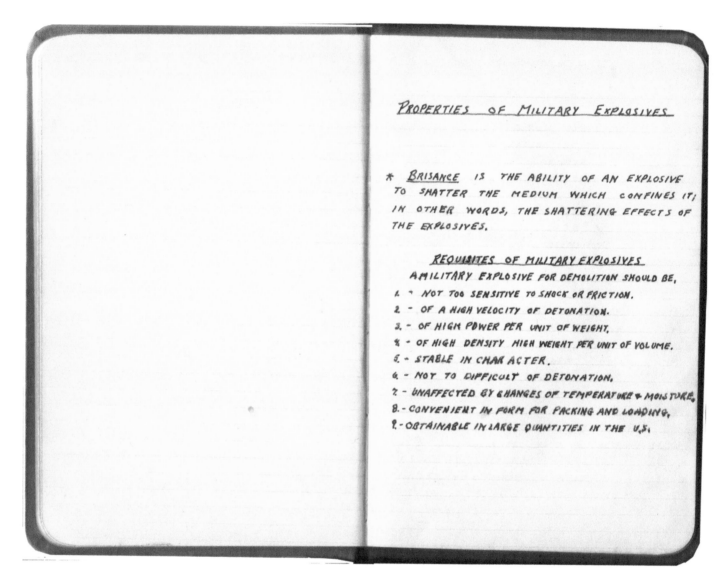

PROPERTIES OF MILITARY EXPLOSIVES

* <u>BRISANCE</u> IS THE ABILITY OF AN EXPLOSIVE TO SHATTER THE MEDIUM WHICH CONFINES IT; IN OTHER WORDS, THE SHATTERING EFFECTS OF THE EXPLOSIVES.

REQUISITES OF MILITARY EXPLOSIVES

A MILITARY EXPLOSIVE FOR DEMOLITION SHOULD BE,

1. * NOT TOO SENSITIVE TO SHOCK OR FRICTION.
2. - OF A HIGH VELOCITY OF DETONATION.
3. - OF HIGH POWER PER UNIT OF WEIGHT.
4. - OF HIGH DENSITY HIGH WEIGHT PER UNIT OF VOLUME.
5. - STABLE IN CHARACTER.
6. - NOT TO DIFFICULT OF DETONATION.
7. - UNAFFECTED BY CHANGES OF TEMPERATURE + MOISTURE.
8. - CONVENIENT IN FORM FOR PACKING AND LOADING.
9. - OBTAINABLE IN LARGE QUANTITIES IN THE U.S.

I used my log notebook for recording the methods and materials we used to do our work. In this volume, I have a step-by-step recipe book for using over thirty types of explosive compounds that we employed in various forms for different purposes throughout the war. While you can probably find some of this information today on the Internet, the details of exactly how we used these compounds is not readily available. We were the first of the Navy commandos and thus, we made many practical discoveries about the cleverest ways to use these materials in the field and under water. What we learned was not published in text books, and the expertise we developed through trial and error under fire is still in use by today's Navy SEALs. For this reason, I include just a few pages for publication in this book. The rest will remain undisclosed.

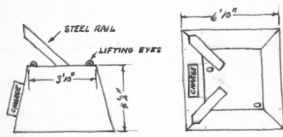

STEEL RAIL

LIFTING EYES

6' 10"

3' 10"

4' 2"

CHARGE

CHARGE

CHARGE

S PACKS ON SEAWARD FACE OF OBSTACLE,

TETRYTAL DEMOLITION PACK CONSISTS OF A CANVAS
BAG CONTAINING EIGHT TNT DEMO. BLOCKS. THE
DIMENSIONS OF THE BLOCK ARE 2" x 11" AND WEIGH
2½ LBS. EACH BLOCK IS RECTRONGULAR IN SHAPE AND
IS WRAPPED IN PAPER BACKED, ASSPHALT IMPREGNATED
CRINCKLE-CRAFT PAPER. THE BLOCKS ARE COMPOSED OF
CAST TETRYTAL WHICH IS 75 PERCENT TETRYL AND
25 PERCENT TNT. THE DIMENSIONS OF THE PACK
CONTAINING 8 BLOCKS ARE APPROXIMATILY 4⅝" THICK,
x 9" WIDE x 11⅜" HIGH. ONE PACK APPROXIMATILY 22 LBS.
THE BLOCKS ARE NOT AFFECTED BY MOISTURE AND
WILL WITHSTAND SUBMERSION IN WATER FOR 24 HRS.
WITHOUT APPRECIABLE EFFECT UPON THEIR CHARACTERISTICS.

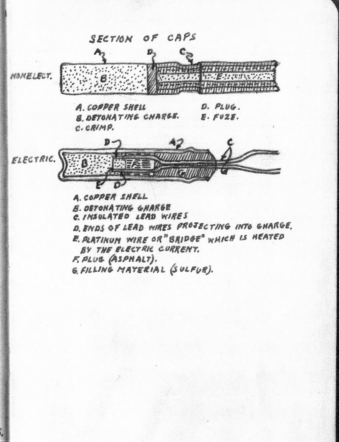

SECTION OF CAPS

NONELECT.

A. COPPER SHELL
B. DETONATING CHARGE.
C. CRIMP.
D. PLUG.
E. FUZE.

ELECTRIC.

A. COPPER SHELL
B. DETONATING CHARGE
C. INSULATED LEAD WIRES
D. ENDS OF LEAD WIRES PROJECTING INTO CHARGE.
E. PLATINUM WIRE OR "BRIDGE" WHICH IS HEATED
   BY THE ELECTRIC CURRENT.
F. PLUG (ASPHALT).
G. FILLING MATERIAL (SULFUR).

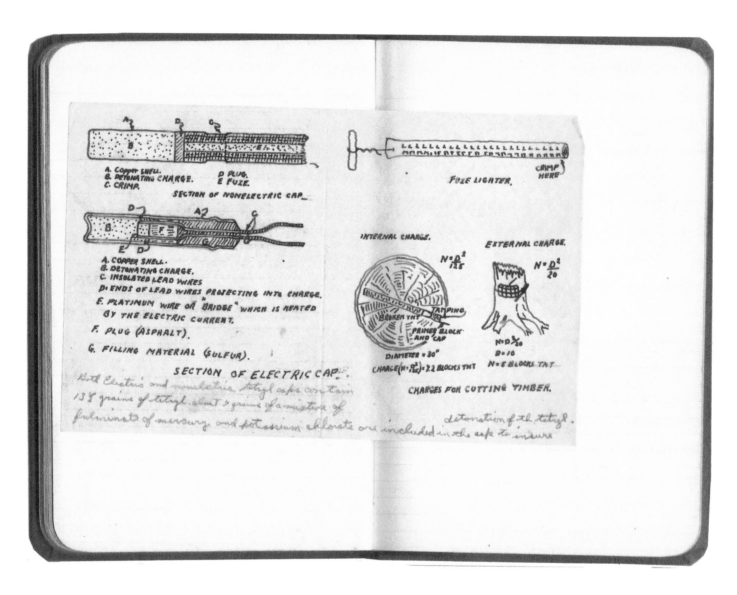

A. Copper Shell.
B. Detonating Charge.
C. Crimp.
D Plug.
E Fuze.

SECTION OF NONELECTRIC CAP

A. COPPER SHELL.
B. DETONATING CHARGE.
C. INSULATED LEAD WIRES
D. ENDS OF LEAD WIRES PROJECTING INTO CHARGE.
E. PLATINUM WIRE OR "BRIDGE" WHICH IS HEATED BY THE ELECTRIC CURRENT.
F. PLUG (ASPHALT).
G. FILLING MATERIAL (SULFUR).

SECTION OF ELECTRIC CAP

FUZE LIGHTER.

CRIMP HERE

INTERNAL CHARGE.
EXTERNAL CHARGE.

$N = \frac{D^2}{125}$

$N = \frac{D^2}{20}$

BROKEN TNT
TAMPING
PRIMER BLOCK AND CAP
DIAMETER = 30"
CHARGE $(N = \frac{D^2}{125}) = 7.2$ BLOCKS TNT

$N = D \times \frac{3}{80}$
$D = 10$
$N = 5$ BLOCKS TNT

CHARGES FOR CUTTING TIMBER.

Both Electric and nonelectric tetryl caps contain 13.5 grains of tetryl. about 5 grains of a mixture of fulminate of mercury and potassium chlorate are included in the cap to insure detonation of the tetryl.

Chapter 4
Cooling It In Coolangatta

We made it to Australia eventually. It only took the better part of a month. When we arrived, clearly, there was no urgency to put us to use. We had raced through training only to sit in Australia for a month.

We arrived in Brisbane, Australia on November 27, 1943 en route to duty under the Seventh Fleet Amphibious Force Commander, Vice Admiral Daniel Barbey. He served under Admiral Thomas Kinkaid, Commander of the entire Seventh Fleet. The whole thing eventually reported up to General MacArthur, the Supreme Allied Commander of the South West Pacific area. It was clearly a big operation, yet when we got to Australia, we couldn't even find the fleet. No one we talked to knew what to do with us.

Back row: Alar Pierce, Frank Kaine, and Sam Pahdopony.
Front Row: Dillard Williams, Harrison Eskridge, and Johnny Wilhide.

In Australia as elsewhere, the NCDU and their capabilities were unknown. Bill's unit, like their counterparts in England, lacked administrative clout. They simply had to wait for further orders and transportation, idling in Australia until shortly after Christmas.

Within short order, a U.S. Army Colonel contacted LTjg Kaine and requested that he come to the flagship "to give a little talk on your capabilities to a group tomorrow morning."

A flagship in the U.S. Navy is one that carries the staff and headquarters of a task force commander, generally an officer holding the rank of admiral. Admirals fly a blue flag with white stars indicating their rank—one, two, three or four stars—at their headquarters and on their staff cars—hence the terms "flag officer" and "flagship."

This "group" on the flagship, which LTjg Kaine thought would be 30 or 40 people, turned out to be what looked like to him to be an entire division of perhaps 1,000 personnel. They were actually elements of the U.S. Army 32nd Division, who the NCDUs would subsequently support as they were working their way up to New Guinea, the Philippines, and Borneo. Many of the personnel out-ranked him.

LTjg Kaine's "little talk" was a success and NCDU's days of waiting were soon over.

His counterpart, Lieutenant Junior Grade Lloyd Anderson was the officer in charge of NCDU-3, which operated in combination with Bill's unit. He attended a meeting in Brisbane with LTjg Kaine, where they were apprised of a plan for NCDU involvement across the Southwest Pacific.

Members of Special Services Unit #1 also attended the meeting in Brisbane. SSU-1 was a newly established Joint and Combined Pacific Scout and Raider commando unit that organized indigenous guerillas to fight against the Japanese. It included U.S. Navy, Army, Marines, and Australian members.

As LTjg Kaine related some years later, "We were just little pipsqueaks in the whole big pattern out there."

LTjg Frank Kaine

LTjg Frank Kaine, who headed my unit, was the most senior officer of all NCDUs in the Pacific. With him was LTjg Lloyd Anderson, officer in charge of NCDU-3. The two of them worked closely together throughout the war.

LTjg Kaine did quite a bit of talking to the top brass once we got to Australia. He had to explain what we did and how the disaster at Tarawa didn't need to happen again. He told them we could go in, chart the reefs and beaches, then blow clear channels for the invading forces. I always got a kick out of thinking of our lieutenant *junior grade* going in to lecture a room full of generals and admirals about where the coral was off the shores of the invasion beaches. It was after the war that we became known as "MacArthur's Frogmen," even though none of us ever had a pair of fins.

LTjg Kaine and LTjg Anderson were big on secrecy. We never learned anything about where we were going until we shoved off and ended up someplace. Only the top brass knew who we were and what we did. We attracted a little attention whenever we went aboard any ship, because we always came on carrying all those explosives. We made the crews pretty uncomfortable, but most of the time, they knew better than to ask us too many questions.

Before we knew what we were doing—before anyone else knew what we were doing—we had plenty of time to kill. We made good use of the time we spent waiting we for orders after we discovered a beach town not far from Brisbane called Coolangatta. We spent most of our liberty there. They had a pretty nice boardwalk, with a variety of activities and entertainment. The beach was nice and the women were even nicer. And no mosquitos sand fleas!

James Sandy and I found a place in Coolangata where we could stay out of trouble.

Conducting beach reconnaissance in Coolangata.

69

COOLENGATA,—AUSTRALIA, DEC. 14, 1943.

Chapter 5
Blowing Reefs in New Guinea

We set off for Townsville, a port north of Brisbane, the day after Christmas 1943. It didn't feel like Christmas at all. In addition to the sunny summer weather, we were finally going to war.

We didn't stay long at that port. Two days after our arrival, we were on the *USS Fulton* headed for Milne Bay in New Guinea. The little we knew about that place was from news reports from just over a year previous about the terrible battle there in September 1942. That was the first time the Allies delivered a decisive defeat to Japan.

We arrived in New Guinea on January 3, 1944 and were sent to a place called Dawa Dawa, a small military camp where we finally reported in. We were reunited with friends in NCDUs 19, 20, and 21 who came in on the *USS James Rolph*. We were glad to see some familiar faces.

New Guinea has two seasons: The rainy season and the really rainy season. We arrived at the height of the really rainy season. I felt a little homesick in that damp jungle and pasted a little poem in my log that ended: "Who wants a place like Guinea when there is the good old U.S.A.?"

LTjg Kaine reported in to a U.S. Marine Corps Colonel. I don't know what it was. Maybe he had heard something about us and couldn't believe we were tougher than his Leathernecks. In any case, the first thing he did was order us on a 36 mile hike through the jungle. He meant to keep us in training or kill us. We didn't complain; we just did it. If any of us felt the slightest bit of fatigue, we sure didn't let him know.

Six NCDUs (2, 3, 19, 20, 21, and after Normandy, NCDU-24), 36 men in total, served with the Seventh Amphibious Force throughout the war, clearing beaches and boat channels from Biak to Borneo. They were the only men to remain as NCDUs for the entire war's duration.

In combination, these NCDUs supported over 36 amphibious assaults and demolition operations, and remained deployed for a period exceeding two years' time.

There wasn't much time for lounging. We trained as hard in New Guinea as we had in Fort Pierce and

DAWSON

A rubber boat was the most comfortable place I could find to nap after our 36-mile jungle hike in New Guinea.

learned how to thrive in the jungle. We knew we were going to be at the front of a major invasion. The plan was that we would go in at night with diving gear to clear a path to the beach. We spent quite a bit of time on night training dives.

We learned to sleep in the jungle. They gave us jungle hammocks. They proved to be complicated to put up, hot as hell, and didn't do anything to keep the bugs off you. We just slept on the ground.

Our uniform evolved to what worked best for whatever environment we encountered. Usually we wore long green khaki pants with rubber soled canvas footwear called jungle boots. We wore those jungle boots all the time—especially swimming.

In all the years we were in the Pacific, none of us ever owned a pair of fins, so we were not technically frogmen in that sense. Instead, we learned to swim with those jungle boots. They kept us from getting cut up by the coral. The coral was so sharp, it would slice into you like a razor and get infected quick. We wore our long pants, because some coral was so soft you would sink into it almost to your waist. You didn't always know what you were getting into, so you learned to appreciate long pants no matter what. We got used to swimming fully clothed so it didn't bother us a bit.

Our first operation was at the Admiralties in March 1944. Like every operation we would go on, we were out in front of everything. As soon as we got the summons, the Australian ship *HMAS Westralia* took us out to LST

DAWSON

Jungle hammocks were more trouble than they were worth, but this one made for a nice photograph.

DAWSON WILHIDE

WILLIAMS KAINE ARMSTRONG

NCDU-2 didn't get a graduation picture, but we did get this. Here we are in New Guinea, ready for action: Dillard Williams, me, Frank Kaine, Johnny Wilhide, and William Armstrong.

SSU-1 had been dispatched from Fergusson Island to the small camp at Milne Bay and then to Dawa Dawa. Their arrival was intended to create an Amphibious Force command structure for special units. NCDUs 2, 3, 19, 20, 21, and eventually NCDU-24 from operations in Europe, were assigned to work in conjunction with the SSU personnel; an arrangement that would serve the NCDU men throughout the war. Lieutenants Lloyd Anderson, OIC of NCDU-3 and Robert Eiring, OIC of NCDU-19, served as instructors for SSU-1.

SSU-1 was a second and lesser-known Scout and Raider group established in the Pacific on 7 July 1943 in Cairns Base in Queensland, Australia. The focus of this outfit was much different from their Atlantic counterparts, which concentrated only on amphibious-assault missions. SSU-1 men collected intelligence, trained and operated with indigenous personnel, and conducted many guerrilla-warfare missions. They were later reorganized and designated the Seventh Amphibious Scouts and organized under shipboard staff intelligence sections.

We frequently had to scrounge for equipment. Here is Johnny Wilhide with one of the flat-bottom wooden boats we were able to acquire—these were easier to use than rubber boats for hauling explosive hose.

We trained on those wooden run-abouts. We trained all the time. We didn't know what we would be called to do or when, but we made it our business to be always ready. It is why I am still here!

SANDY WILLIAMS

ARMSTRONG, PAHDOPONY, WILLIAMS   ESKRIDGE
PIERCE   DAWSON

Here we are after another one of those long, hot jungle hikes.

ARMSTRONG

WILHIDE   KAINE   DAWSON

Our two units, mine, NCDU-2, commanded by Frank Kaine (right) and NCDU-3, commanded by Lloyd Anderson (left), worked together closely.

ANDERSON   KAINE

Here is how we typically looked when getting ready to go on a mission. NCDU-3 included James Sandy, Constantius DeVries, Lloyd Anderson, Edward Messall, and Harrison Eskridge.

466, (LST refers to Landing Ship, Tank.) The LST was already underway, which meant we had to load it out in the open sea, which complicated the operation. We all worked together, officers and men, through the night to mule-haul our explosives aboard. I have to tell you, we sure made the sailors nervous as they watched us load tons and tons of explosives on their ship.

When we made Hyane Harbor on the east side of Manus Island on March 23, we were given an LCM or Landing Craft, Medium to work from. The trouble was, no one could find anyone that knew what they wanted us to do or what we could do. In due time, someone did find an officer in the U.S. Navy Beachmaster's office, who had a task for us.

He told us "We have to blow this reef out of here. You guys said you can do this. You've got to do it, because we've got reinforcements coming in tomorrow morning or the next morning."

We answered, "Good, no problem."

No problem except we didn't really know whether we could do it or not. Still, it was something to to occupy us and we sure didn't want to be sitting around.

A couple of us surveyed the reef while swimming among schools of sharks and other large fish. It looked to be about twelve feet thick, which was pretty feasible in our estimation.

We used Bangalore torpedoes. Instead of taking them out of their boxes, we simply hooked in the explosive-laden crates with rope, one every three feet.

Name _____ DAWSON, William Louis
(Name in Full. Surname to the Left)

256 52 66 Rate_____ GM3c
(Service No.)

Date Reported Aboard:_____ 9 September 1943

Naval Combat Demolition Unit No. 2
(Present Ship or Station)

_____ # 1 _____ (Ship or Station Received From)

9 March to 23 March 1944:
Participated with credit in the operation against Japanese forces at Admiralty Islands, Bismarck Archipelago.

F.R. Kaine
O-in-C, NCDU #2

_____ # 2

19-24 April 1944:
Participated at Tanah-Merah, Humboldt Bay, Aitape, New Guinea operation against Japanese forces.

F.R. Kaine
O-in-C, NCDU #2

Date Transferred _____

To _____

_____
Signature and Rank of Commanding Officer

Date Received Aboard:_____

_____
(New Ship or Station)

_____
(Last Ship or Station)

_____
Signature and Rank of Commanding Officer

ORIGINAL
FOR SERVICE RECORD

NDCU-2 and NCDU-3's first operation was at the Admiralty Islands 200 miles north of New Guinea. The Admiralties, once a Dutch domain, retained place names given by colonial authorities. They had been occupied by the Japanese since 1942. General MacArthur planned to invade the Admiralties in a division-size operation on 1 April 1944, but air reconnaissance in February indicated the islands were lightly defended. Ignoring the estimates of his intelligence staff that there were several thousand Japanese troops in the islands, who would likely put up stiff resistance, MacArthur decided to gamble and advance the landing to the end of February, even though all the forces earmarked for the operation would not be ready by that point. He planned to land a reconnaissance force on Los Negros and then rush in reinforcements faster than the Japanese could react.

The Admiralties operation began on 29 February with the landing of troops from the 1st Cavalry Division at Lorengau Beach. There were several thousand Japanese on Los Negros, and it turned out to be an unexpected fight against a large contingent of Imperial Japanese Marines. MacArthur's forces had to reinforce and bring in more troops to drive them out. The NCDU men were not actually used ahead of time for the pre-assault operations, leaving U.S. forces in the dark. It was discovered that the 1st Cavalry Division couldn't be reinforced as planned except from the backside of the island at Hyane Harbor. The harbor had a natural entrance that came up to the shore on both sides, and was perhaps a half-mile across; however, in the middle was a submerged reef only about 20 feet under the surface. The Navy ships carrying the reinforcements drew 26-30 feet when fully loaded. Battle planners sent for the NCDU men, who were still in New Guinea.

We figured that would give us enough blasting power to get the job done all at once. Once we rigged the reef with the crates of explosives, we ran our detonation cord from box to box and placed blasting caps in each one. We worked all day until pitch black night and again the next morning in depths of 20 feet, wearing our green coveralls and jungle boots as protection against the live coral. By the time we finished, we had laid a blanket of demolitions over the entire reef, across the top and down both sides.

Finally the time came to make the shot. When we got ready to fire an explosive charge, we would always yell out, "Fire in the hole!" and wait a few seconds before hitting the detonator.

The Bangalore torpedoes used by NCDU-2 and NCDU-3 were not actually torpedoes. They were five-foot long explosive tube charges, which could be connected to each other at either end. Each tube contained a little over nine pounds of high explosives. Ten Bangalore torpedoes were contained in one box. These demolition charges could be used by the NCDUs to clear obstacles that would otherwise require them to approach the obstruction directly, possibly under fire. Placing the Bangalore torpedos, still in their boxes, to create a blanket of demolitions was quite ingenious.

The twelve of us had emplaced 47 tons of demolitions, and when that shot went off, the slap on the bottom of our boat felt like it could almost fracture our feet. The explosion looked like it was in slow motion at first, but it shot up a huge water flume. We took that as a good sign, because it indicated that all of our munitions had exploded.

After the water settled, we went in to see how effective we had been. The water was too deep to investigate while free diving, so we used surface swimming techniques with lead lines. We measured the depth to be 47 feet – not bad as we were shooting for 30 feet. It was definitely, "good, no problem," as we had promised, which was fortunate. By the time we finished examining the reef; we looked out to sea and saw the first ship with reinforcements already coming in.

What success looked like for NCDU-2.

Blowing that reef immediately established our reputation. It was our first operation, so we felt very good about what we had done.

Our two units stayed together through the whole war, taking turns with the other NCDUs for operations most of the time. Sometimes we would work together as a pair of units when the job was too big for just one.

The actions and activities of the NCDU men on this operation were so significant that the story was later mentioned in T*ime Magazine.*

LTjg Kaine, as the senior officer of all the NCDU groups in our area, would go off and get the orders, often two or three operations at one time. He would then figure out who was going to which one.

We were usually transported to the assault area by an LSD, or Landing Ship, Dock. Then we would embark on an LCI or Landing Craft, Infantry, or an APD, which was an old cut-down four stack destroyer turned into a high-speed transport for personnel.

Adding to the difficulty of our operations was the fact that most of the existing sailing charts were

What the 36 men of the six Pacific NCDUs did in the Seventh Amphibious Force was somewhat different from work done by the other Fort Pierce NCDUs. Those other units had been formed into 100-man UDTs at the Naval Combat Demolition Unit Training and Experimental Base at Maui.

LT Kaine's Pacific NCDUs remained individual five-man, one officer units, and thus, maintained their identity as NCDUs throughout the war. They never combined into one unit like the UDTs. These six NCDUs operated in pairs. The Navy leadership that Bill's unit worked for, the Seventh Amphibious Force, thought that they'd have more coverage and better mileage by keeping them as separate entities and operating two at a time for each beach reconnaissance or demolition mission.

The NCDU officers strived for parity between the units as to the number of landings since, among other things, they were worried about the men getting injured or getting nervous disorders, hypertensive, or depressed. This was because they were out there alone in the front of the invasions and were far away from home. They were going to get the war done. The NCDU officers were going to keep the same teams and operate each as a team; that was how they were going to win the war. With that in mind, the goal was to alternate landings.

They didn't know it at the time, but these three NCDU pairs of 36 men would participate in a total of 36 landings over a period of two years, which had them in a one-in-three rotation. Sometimes the Amphibious Force would conduct two landings at the same time, and in one instance they participated in one landing that had three assaults at the same time, so all three combined units (all 36 men), were used.

only accurate within a mile. That was significant when swimming was involved, or when a beach area was completely unknown. It fell to us to go in ahead of the assault forces to conduct a hydrographic reconnaissance of the target beaches, and to make sure they were not mined or booby trapped.

We captured an awful lot of flags! With the big ships' guns going off over our heads, we would swim into Japanese camps and take what they had left.

WILLIAM SANDY

DAWSON PIERCE ARMSTRONG

DAWSON PIERCE

We didn't just capture flags--we almost always found saki, too. You know the enemy had left in a hurry if they left us their booze.

A Landing Craft, Personnel Ramp, or LCPR, loaded with our rubber boats, would maneuver in as close as possible. Then we would launch our boats and paddle in the rest of the way to complete our mission. We would paddle toward the beach until we started taking enemy fire or as close as we thought to be a safe distance. We would then drop anchor and swim the rest of the way in. Sometimes we had explosives with us.

I remember one time we took fire. We all jumped out of the rubber boat and took cover behind it. I looked at my swim buddy and we started laughing that we were using a rubber inflatable boat filled with TNT as our "cover." We must have had an angel looking out for us that time. I hate to think what would have happened if we had taken a round.

Once we got in to shore close enough to swim, or if we started getting fired upon, the Navy destroyers behind us would open up their five-inch guns over our heads aimed directly at the beaches. The noise was deafening. You would think that would be frightening, but we actually took great comfort when the ships began these barrages. No one ever shot at us when the ship's guns were blazing.

We got shot at often. And we were scared quite a bit. Anyone who says they were not scared is a damn fool or a liar. I was scared quite a few times and I don't mind admitting it. Anyone in my position would be scared. Sometimes it was rifle fire, and sometimes it was mortar fire. We always felt safe in the sea. We learned that we were hardly visible when in the water, because only our heads were exposed. Even in calm conditions, it was very hard to see us with the naked eye, and we were very careful to swim without splashing. We had the benefit of surprise too. The enemy didn't expect a half dozen men to swim up on them in the dark of night.

We did a lot of beach reconnaissance. The charts we had were not very good, so it was our job to fill in the gaps. We would form a line of swimmers parallel to the beach, generally in 25-yard intervals. These reconnaissance operations usually required that two NCDUs, a total of 12 men, work together. Each of us had a slate and lead pencil—a low tech solution to writing underwater. We would then take "soundings" using a small knotted line with a weight on the end. We tied knots in those lines in one-foot intervals, another low tech solution that gave us a pretty accurate way of measuring the depth of the water. When we combined the soundings of the survey, we had a good profile of the beach gradient and would know whether or not we needed to get about blowing things up.

When we found reefs or sandbars, we would return the next day to accomplish the demolition work. We used either rubber hose or Bangalore torpedoes. The rubber hose came in thirty foot sections with two pounds of TNT per foot. It was very hard work to lug

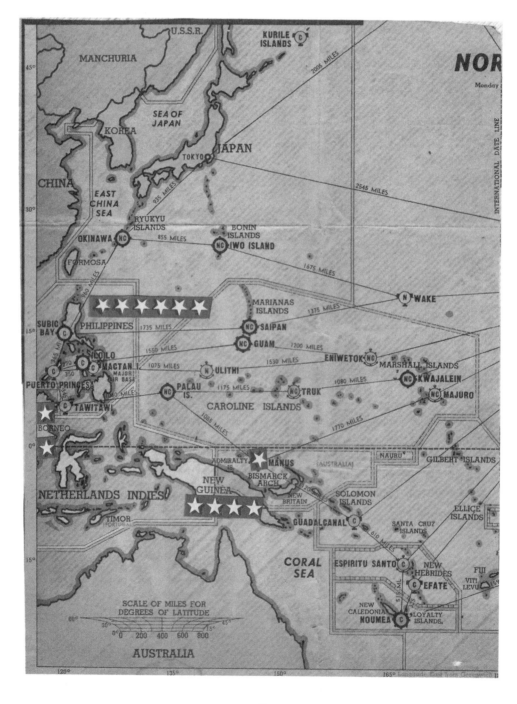

those things around, but then we didn't know any better. In any case, we needed to bet the job done, so there was no point in complaining. We could connect the rubber hose in sections, which we liked to do because it would blow coral reefs and sandbars so evenly. That made the hard work satisfying.

On our dives, we usually used a canvas rebreather rig that came down over our heads. It had a small can of soda lime and a tank of oxygen that was good for about a half an hour. We also had a rig with a hand pump and a hose going to the surface. Those were pretty awkward because you could only go so far and that wasn't good for our work. We covered a lot of ground on our dives and needed to be able to move more freely.

For such small units it would seem that they had very little impact in the war's big picture; however, Bill and his teammates felt that they were a definite part of the war effort, and were leaving their mark. They operated alone for over two-years and sometime felt that they had been forgotten. But, they had a lot of opportunities, and also a lot of slack time. It was not possible to conduct an invasion every day of the week. Each of the combined NCDUs did 12 landings, which resulted in a lot of down time. However, between directed operations, the men trained, maintained their equipment, and would get updates on operating tactics and techniques from Maui or Fort Pierce. They did not have time for boredom.

The coral reefs were so beautiful that it was a shame we had to blow them up. Sometimes, we would take a moment to just go sit on the bottom and watch the fish go by. It was so peaceful down there you could forget that you were at war.

Sometimes those reefs scared you. I remember one where the drop off was pretty steep and the current was swift. It felt like it was going to take you right down into the black. You couldn't see where it ended. We were very careful to hold on tight. You could get lost forever.

We saw all sorts of colorful tropical fish, just like being in an aquarium. We saw sharks and stingrays and the occasional octopus. They didn't bother us and we were not afraid of them.

The only time I was truly nervous was when one of our demolitions didn't go off. We were all in the rubber boat and it was my turn to dive so we could recap it. Just as I was about to go in, a sea snake swam by. It was as big around as our explosive hose and easily 15 feet long. I looked at that snake and then at the guys and they looked at me. We knew these snakes were extremely venomous and were sometimes very aggressive. Still, there was no question I had to dive. I would never let my team down. If I didn't go, one of the others would have to do it and, I couldn't let that happen. So off I went and felt very uneasy about it.

The people were just as interesting as the landscape and the animals. I took quite a few pictures of the people we encountered. They would come out of nowhere and wander through our camp.

Sometimes they wanted to trade. Sometimes they just wanted to see what we were up to. I know we traded for hats, and some of us might have bought a grass skirt or two. The hats we could use on missions. The skirts were not so practical.

The local people were no fans of the Japanese, who often forced them to work. They were always very nice to us and were more than willing to pose for a picture.

Chapter 6
Japanese Manuals and Propaganda

We almost always took the enemy by surprise. When we came ashore, the Japanese went running, leaving everything behind. We captured quite a bit of material that was surely useful to war planners.

The Japanese defenders often left so quickly that we would find half-eaten meals still warm. The beer and saki we always took and always made good use of. The flags we captured were good for a picture and a keepsake.

Some of the more interesting things we found were abandoned manuals that covered everything from sighting a canon to making sure your uniform was worn just right. I was amazed at how carefully the manuals were drawn and labeled. As much attention was given to the proper placement of an officer's stars as to the calibrating their range finders.

ほまれ

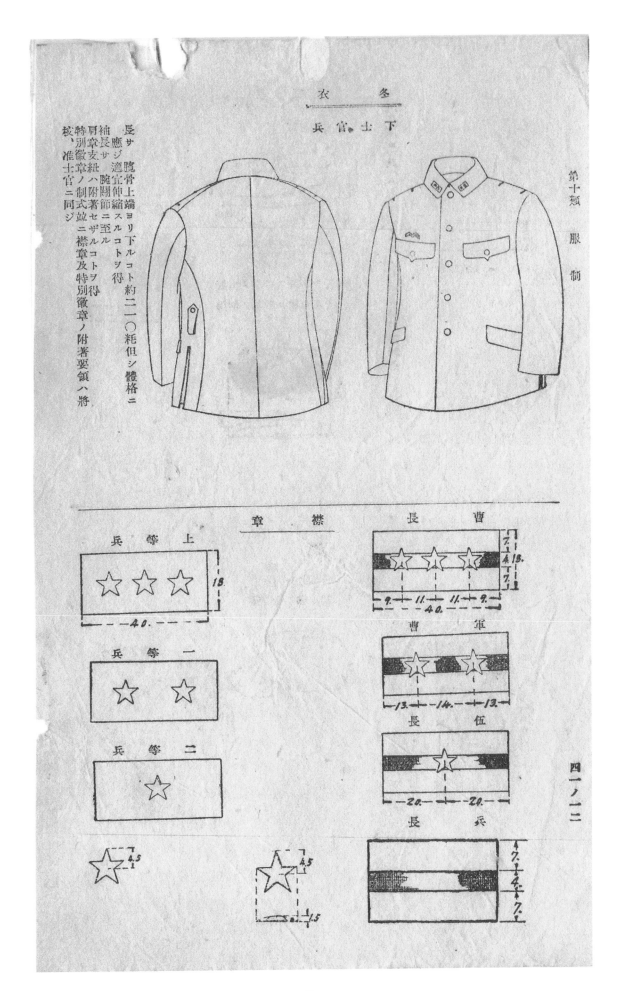

冬衣

下士官兵

襟章

上等兵	曹長	
一等兵	軍曹	
二等兵	伍長	
	兵長	

長サハ腕骨上端ヨリ下ルコト約二一〇粍但シ體格ニ
應ジ適宜伸縮スルコトヲ得
袖長サハ腕關節ニ至ルコトヲ得
肩章、紐ハ附著セザルコトヲ得
特別徽章ノ制式並ニ襟章及特別徽章ノ附著要領ハ將
校、准士官ニ同ジ

四一ノ一二

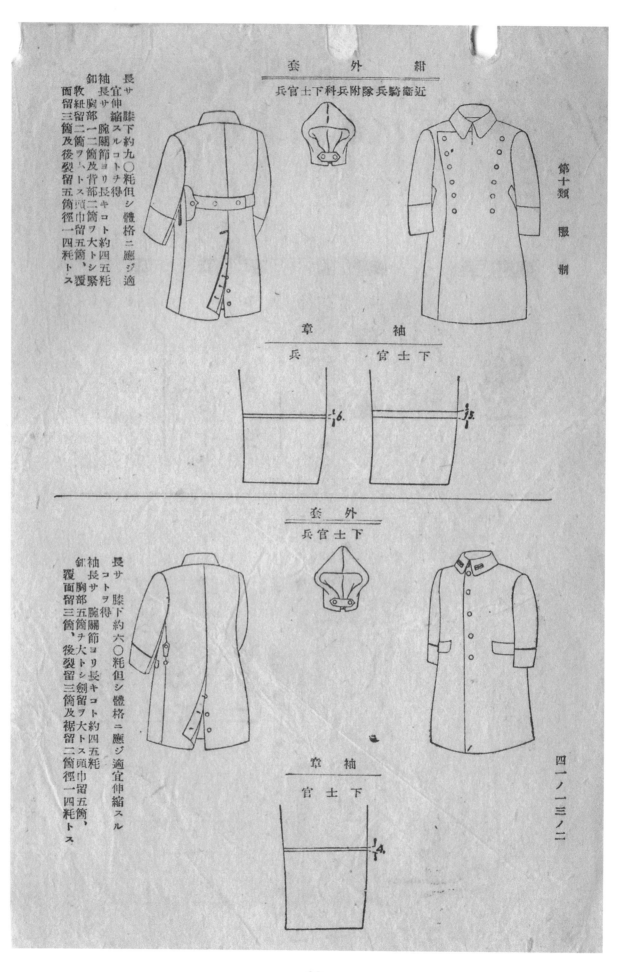

紺 外 套

近衞騎兵隊附兵科下士官兵

第十類 服制

袖 章

兵　　下士官

長サ膝下約九〇糎但シ體格ニ應ジ適
宜伸縮スルコトヲ得但シ體格ニ應ジ適
袖長サ腕關節ヨリ長キコト約四五糎
胸部一二箇及背部二箇ヲ大トシ緊
釦胸部一二箇及背部二箇ヲ大トシ頭巾留五箇、覆
面牧紐留二箇及後裂留五箇徑一四糎トス
留三箇及後裂留五箇徑一四糎トス

外 套

下士官兵

袖 章

下士官

長サ膝下約六〇糎但シ體格ニ應ジ適宜伸縮スル
コトヲ得
袖長サ腕關節ヨリ長キコト約四五糎
胸部五箇ヲ大トシ劍留ヲ大トシ頭巾留五箇、
釦胸部五箇ヲ大トシ頭巾留五箇、覆
面留三箇、後裂留三箇及裾留二箇徑一四糎トス

二ノ三一ノ一四

88

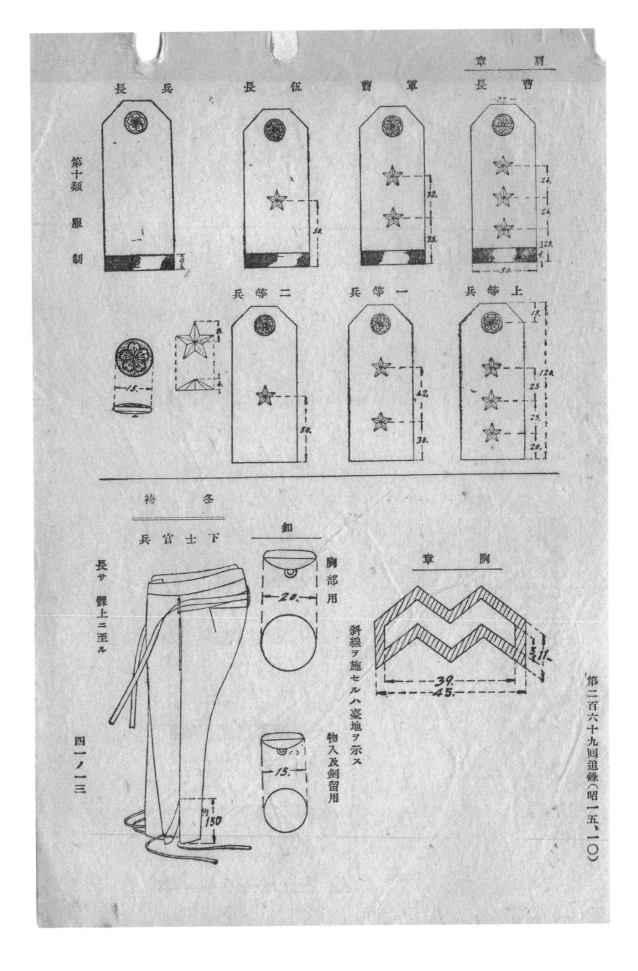

曹 長　　　軍 曹　　　伍 長　　　兵 長

第十類　服制

上 等 兵　　　一 等 兵　　　二 等 兵

冬 袴

下 士 官 兵

長サ　踝上二至ル

四一ノ一三

釦

胸部用

斜線ヲ施セルハ臺地ヲ示ス

物入及劍留用

胸 章

第二百六十九回追錄（昭一五、一〇）

89

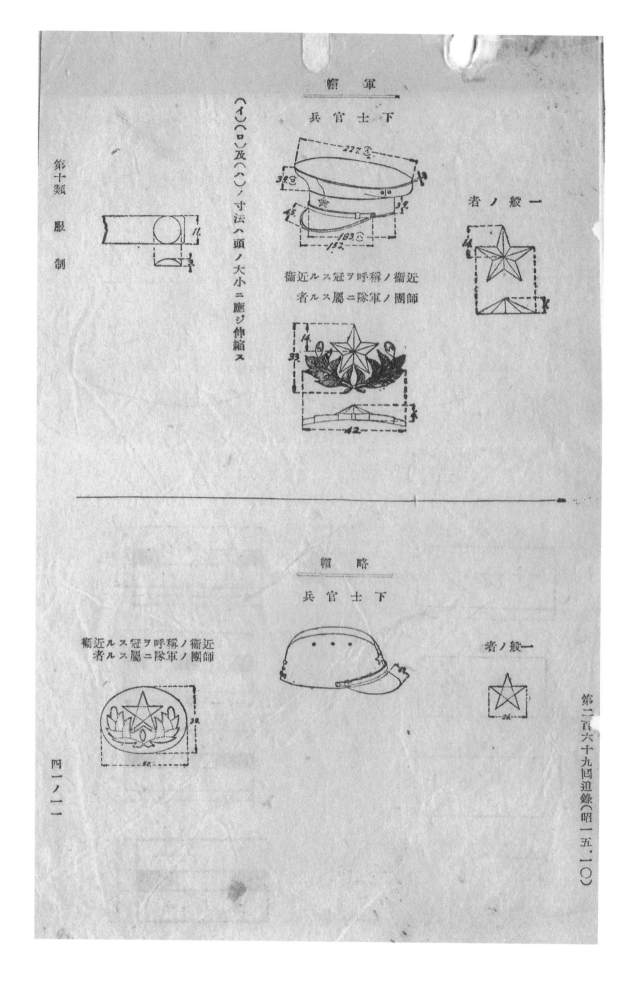

軍帽

下士官兵

一般ノ者

近衛ノ稱呼ヲ冠スル近衛
師團ノ軍隊ニ屬スル者

（イ）（ロ）及（ハ）ノ寸法ハ頭ノ大小ニ應ジ伸縮ス

略帽

下士官兵

一般ノ者

近衛ノ稱呼ヲ冠スル近衛
師團ノ軍隊ニ屬スル者

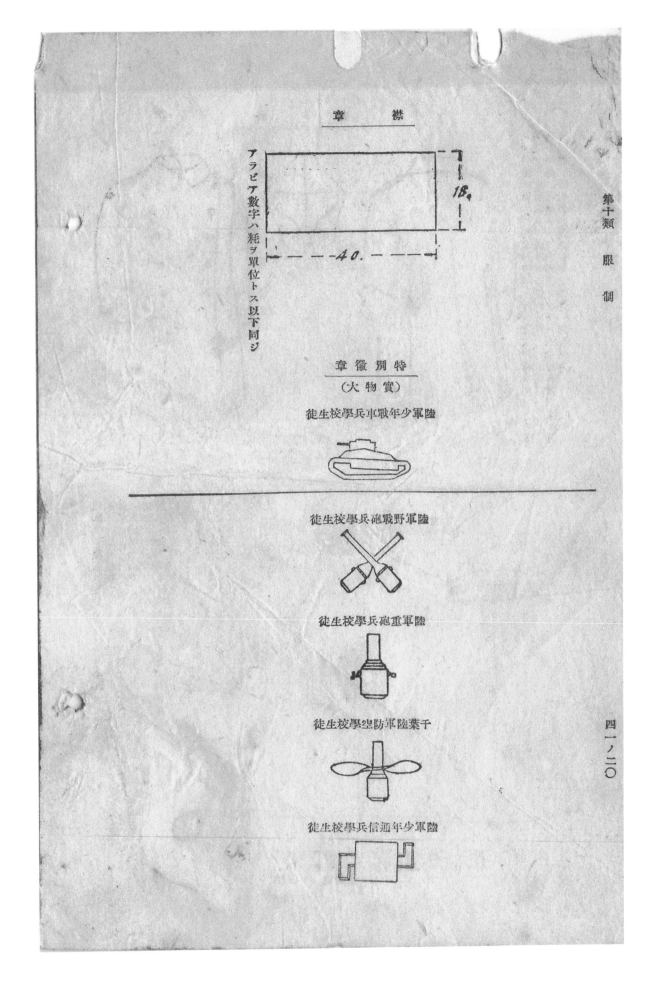

襟章

アラビア數字ハ粍ヲ單位トス以下同ジ

特別徽章
（實物大）

陸軍少年戰車兵學校生徒

陸軍野戰砲兵學校生徒

陸軍重砲兵學校生徒

千葉陸軍防空學校生徒

陸軍少年通信兵學校生徒

九〇式三米測高機名稱圖

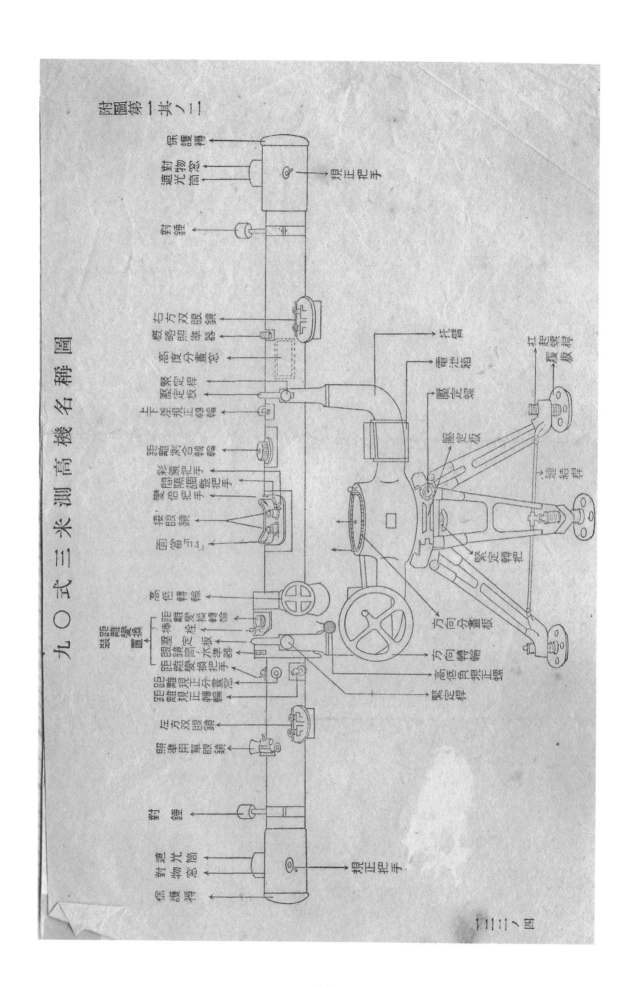

保護蓋
對物窓
遮光筒
規正把手

對錘

右方双眼鏡
概略照準器
高度分畫窓
緊定桿
壓定板
上下差規正轉輪
距離測合轉輪
變眼間隔把手
變倍眼鏡把手
距離調整把手
接眼鏡
國當ラム

托臂
電池箱
壓定螺
壓定板
緊定轉把
方向分畫板

扛起桿
履架桿
連結桿

高低轉輪
高低變換轉輪
距離變換裝置
距離眼鏡插距定栓
距離規正轉輪
距離規正把手
換水板
高低分畫窓
準器

方向轉轉輪
高低角規正螺
緊定桿

左方双眼鏡
照準用單眼鏡

對錘

對物窓
遮光筒
保護蓋

規正把手

眼鏡托架ノ距離變換裝置要領圖

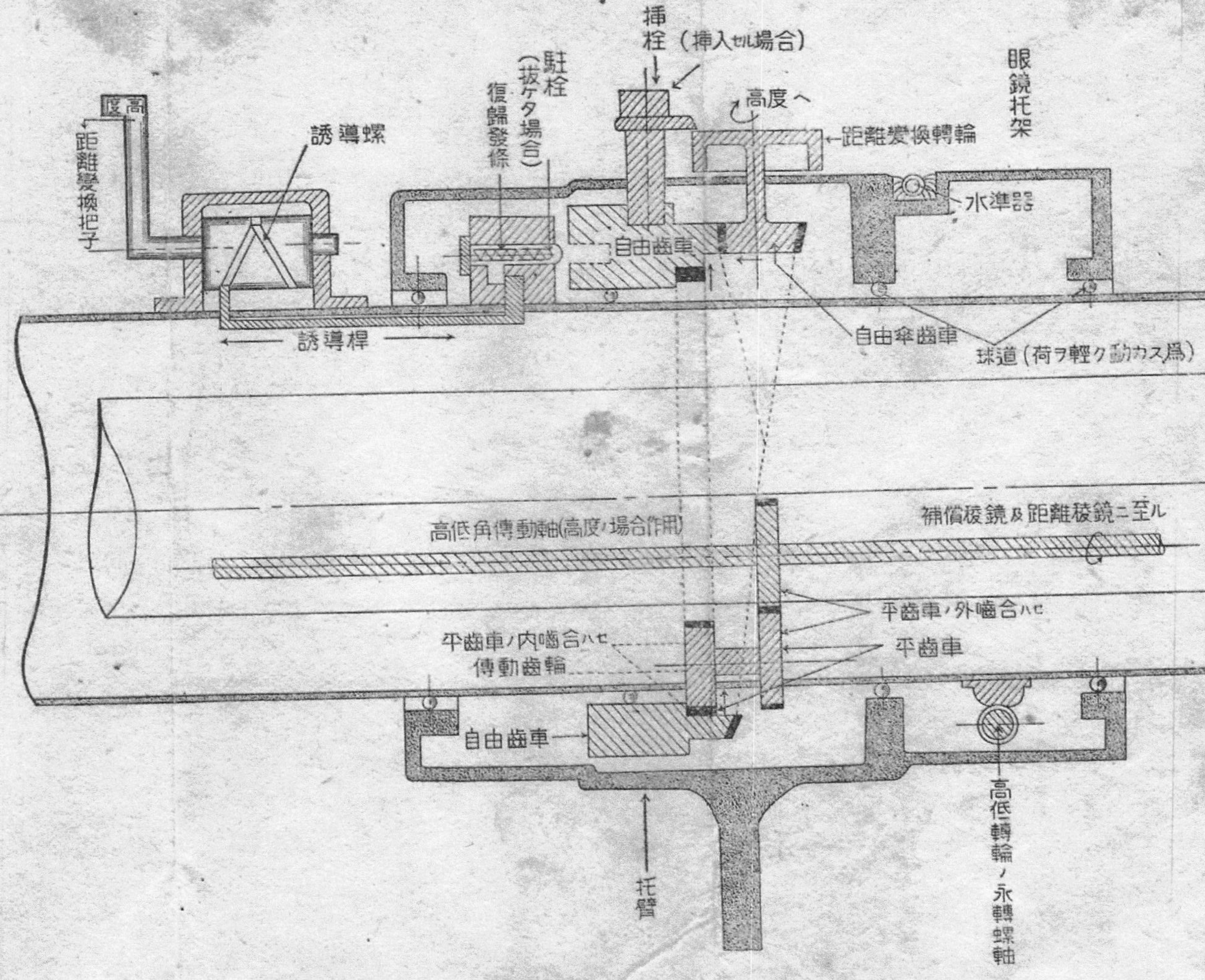

備考

一、本要圖ハ高度（上）傳動齒車ノ高度場合ヲ眼鏡ニ固定セシムルニアリテ誘導車（上）高度ヲ眼鏡ニ示ス

二、傳動齒車ハ高度場合ニ眼鏡ヲ固定セラレテアリ三二八九

93

附圖第三

測高機ノ眼鏡筒右端附近要圖

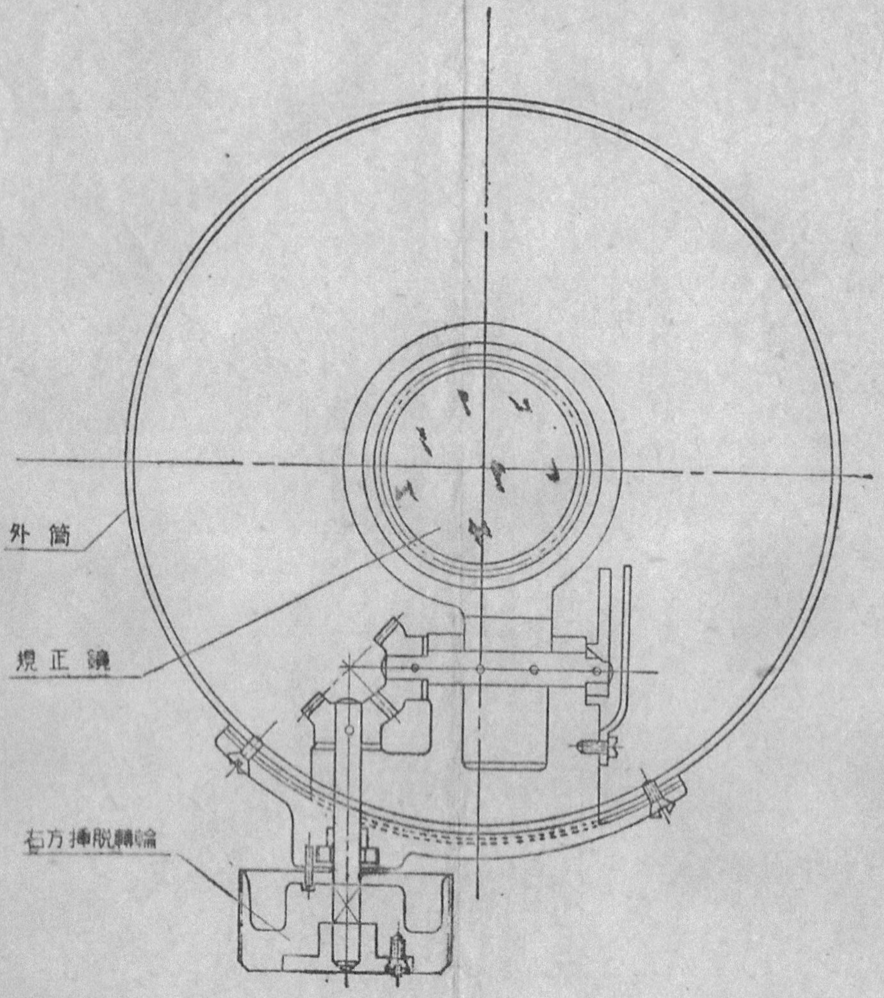

一三二ノ六

We almost always found plenty of propaganda. I never took it seriously. To me, it was like reading the funny pages. Most of us just laughed it off.

The Australian guys didn't think it was that funny. Some of the pages showed Americans in bed with Australian women, while they were out fighting. Somebody sure put a lot of effort into making these flyers.

Some fliers invited us to surrender. No one bought the story that the Japanese were preparing us nice hot meals followed by a ticket home. We couldn't believe that the Japanese believed that anyone would believe them!

★ 投降票 ★

Directions For Surrendering

We guarantee the life of any individual who surrenders voluntarily and presents himself in accorrdance with the following instuctions:

1. Make known your intentions to surrender by displaying a white flag or white cloth, or by waving your hat or hands when approaching the Japanese Army.

2. Bring your rifles and guns with you, slinging them behind your shoulders with the muzzle pointing downwards. Also bring your ammunitions.

3. Present this card to the Japanese Soldier; it will serve as guarantee of your life.

4. This card may be used by one individual or by a group of men.

N O T E : A special consideration will be accorded to those who come to surrender in a large group.

February 1, 1943.
The garrison commander of the Imperial Nippon Forces
(Official seal of the Garrison Commander)

大 日 本 軍 警 備 隊 長

Capt. Edilberto Ramos—Home again and happy together with his family. He had surrendered voluntarily and was released.

That unforgettable embrace under the beautiful moon with the warmth of HER shapely body nestled against yours; that blood-tingling kiss; that over-powering sense of passion that sweeps over you—these and many other pleasant memories you'll be able to relive again if you'll throw down your arms, surrender and prepare to get out of this hell-hole.

This one is clever—the cover has a nice scene—but turn the page...

BUT if you continue to resist ·············
Then, under the beautiful tropical moon, only **DEATH** awaits you.
Bullet-holes in your guts---agonizing death!
You have the two alternatives.

Take your choice.

That unforgettable embrace under the beautiful moon with the warmth of HER shapely body nestled against yours; that blood-tingling kiss, that overpowering sense of passion that sweeps over you—these and many other pleasant memories you'll be able to relive again if you'll throw down your arms, surrender and prepare to get out of this hell-hole.

Here is another example of a fold-over flyer

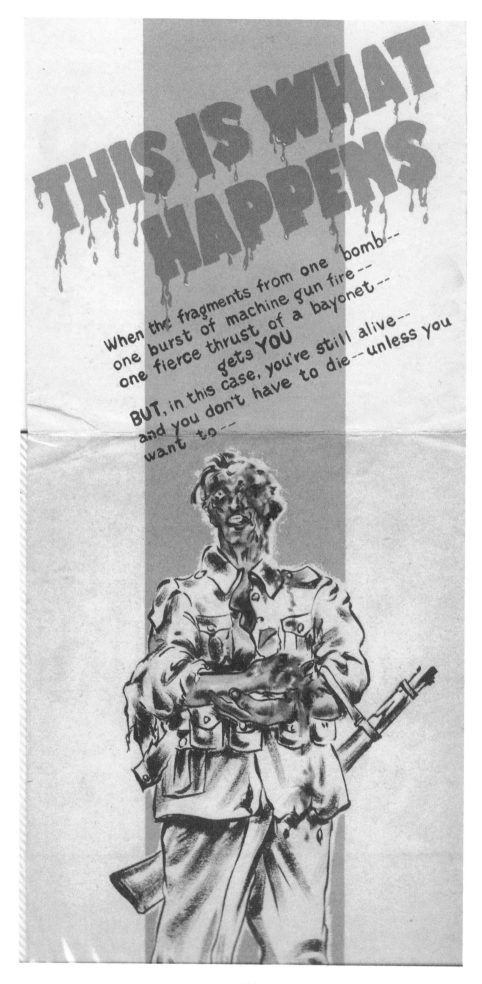

THIS IS WHAT HAPPENS

When the fragments from one bomb--
one burst of machine gun fire--
one fierce thrust of a bayonet--
                        gets YOU

BUT, in this case, you're still alive--
and you don't have to die--unless you
want to--

HELLO, CHAPS !

We sometimes go
on sight, seeing...
Howell

Available as " Passport to Life ".
JAPANESE ARMY HEADQUARTERS
本票持參者ハ投降者ニ付保護ヲ加フベシ
大日本軍司令官

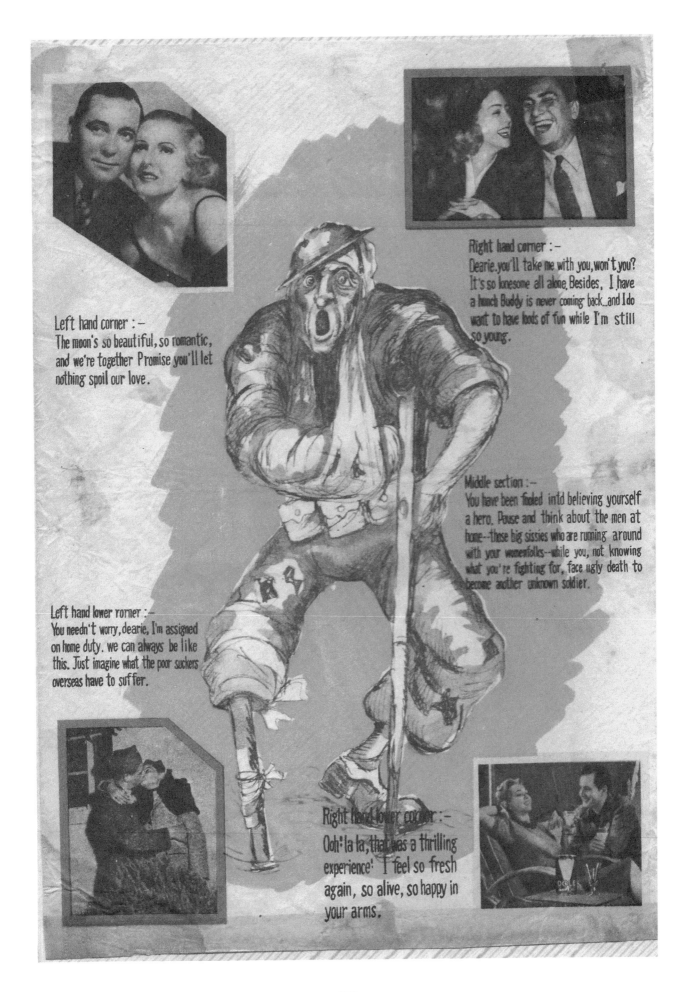

Left hand corner : –
The moon's so beautiful, so romantic, and we're together. Promise you'll let nothing spoil our love.

Right hand corner : –
Dearie, you'll take me with you, won't you? It's so lonesome all alone. Besides, I have a hunch Buddy is never coming back...and I do want to have loods of fun while I'm still so young.

Middle section : –
You have been fooled into believing yourself a hero. Pause and think about the men at home--these big sissies who are running around with your womenfolks--while you, not knowing what you're fighting for, face ugly death to become another unknown soldier.

Left hand lower rorner : –
You needn't worry, dearie, I'm assigned on home duty. we can always be like this. Just imagine what the poor suckers overseas have to suffer.

Right hand lower corner : –
Ooh! la la, that was a thrilling experience! I feel so fresh again, so alive, so happy in your arms.

To All Straggling Soldiers:

Let this fact be known to those straggling soldiers who, having escaped or run into the mountains, are still continuing a futile resistance:

You are no longer soldiers of the USAFFE.

The USAFFE ceased to exist since the 7th of May, 1942, upon the surrender of Lieut.-General Wainwright, and you are nothing but a bunch of bandits.

For what cause or for whose sake, and for how long do you expect to confine yourselves in the mountains?

Are not tens of thousands of Filipino soldiers who became prisoners of war, having received a course of training and instruction, released to return to their homes, and working in happiness together with their families? Do you not think it foolish to continue hiding in the mountains only to be wiped out by the Nippon Imperial Forces, believing foolishly in the false propaganda that you would be killed if you become prisoners of war?

If you leave the mountains and come to surrender you shall have happiness; but if you remain in the mountains and continue this futile and useless resistance, you will be shot to death to the last man.

107

HERE'S ALL YOU DO !

1) Come towards our lines waving a white flag !
2) Strap your gun over your left shoulder, muzzle down and pointed behind you.
3) Show this ticket to the sentry.
4) Any number of you may surrender with this one ticket.

JAPANESE ARMY HEADQUARTERS

通 行 證

本票持參者ハ投降者ニ付保護ヲ加フベシ

大 日 本 軍 司 令 官

110

Iron-rationed. Stranded.
Nothing but dog biscuits
  Day after day, positively.
How about a dish of salad like this?
For a change of diet... just a change of mind.

It's yours for the asking!

It is interesting that the Japanese portrayed President Roosevelt as a virile man standing on two feet.

CITATION

Gen. Douglas MacArthur
C+C S.W. PACIFIC

NEW GUINEA

KILLED IN ACTION!
Died that the jungles of New Guinea
might again rest in peace.

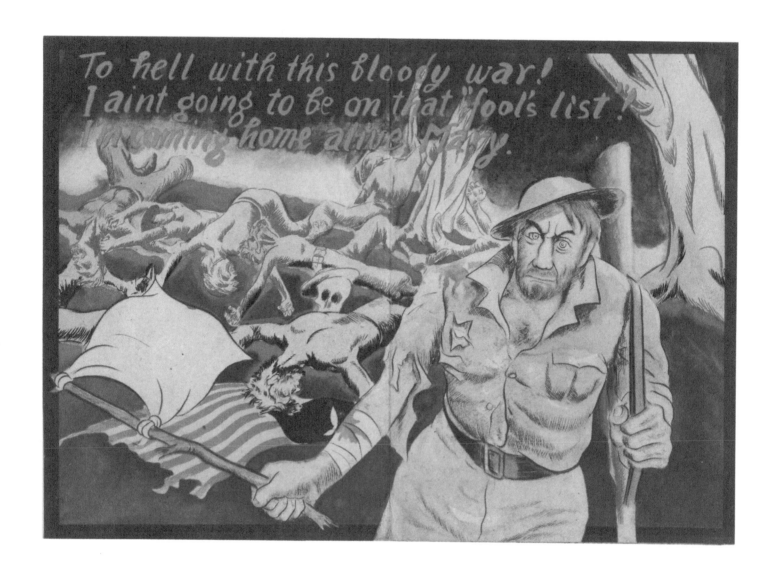

Another "major victory" for the United States!
As champagne glasses clinked around the radio, doughboys
at the front lay cold and lifeless on the bloody wires.
Oh! if those at home only knew what you are undergoing.
But, they'll never know, 'cause the honorable colonel —
secretaries of the Army and Navy won't have it!

Another "major victory" for the United States!
As champagne glasses clinked around the radio, doughboys
at the front lay cold and lifeless on the bloody wires.
Oh! if those at home only knew what you are undergoing.
But they'll never know, 'cause the honorable colonel —
secretaries of the Army and Navy won't have it!

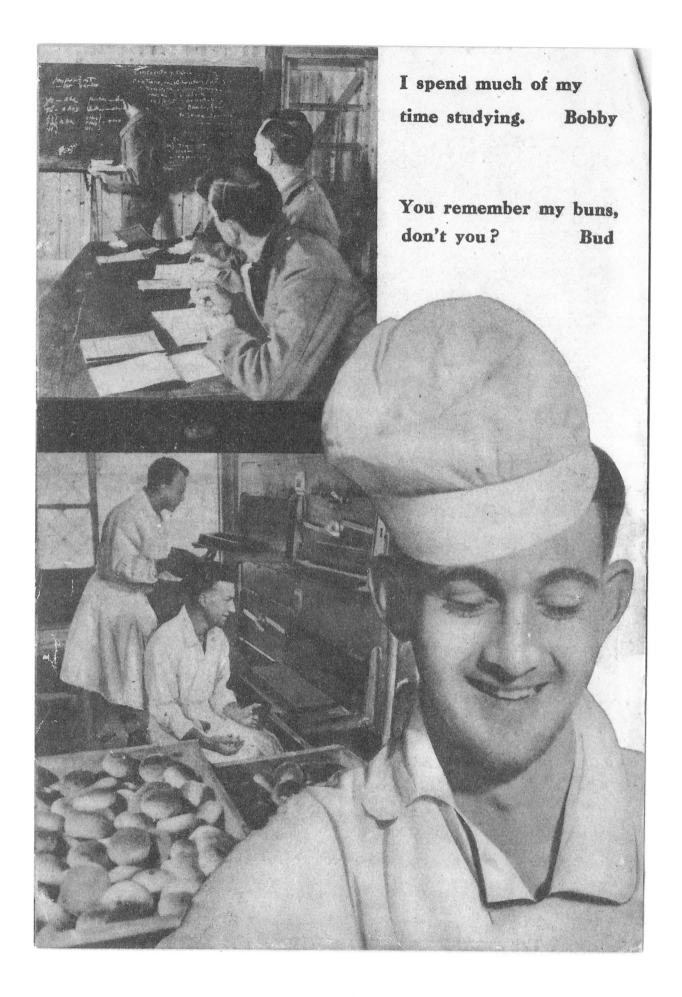

I spend much of my
time studying.   Bobby

You remember my buns,
don't you?   Bud

いなは鬼に間世る渡

戦争をしてゐる時には我々は案外お互びに相手の氣持を良く理解せず又余り深く考へやうとしないものです。

今假りに諸君が米國軍側に來られたとしたならば今まで想像にも及ばなかつた色々な事に接し認識を新たにするのではないでせうか、例ば次の寫眞に現はれてゐる様なことが一つの例です。

（日本家族保護の爲の目隱し）

123

In addition to propaganda, we found quite a bit of scrip and counterfeit money. The Japanese printed invasion money for use during their occupation of various countries and possessions. Some of it is real, and some of it is not.

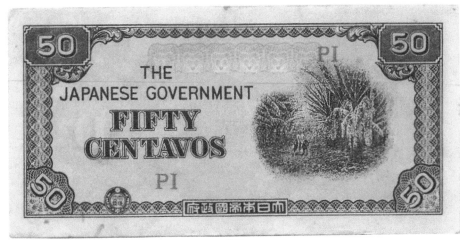

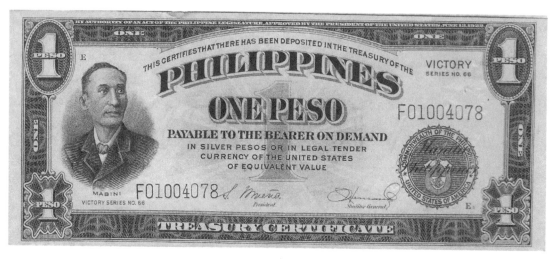

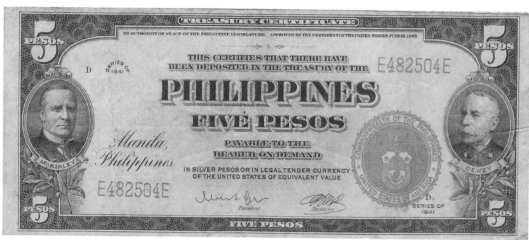

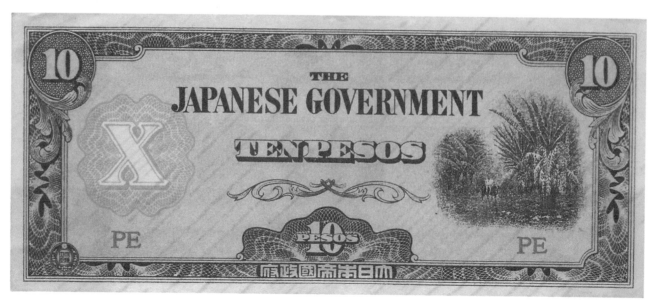

Chapter 7
Plenty of Action

We arrived at Aitape on April 17, 1944 aboard the LST-45. We transfered to YSM-51 for the transit into the port

On the way, we witnessed the arrival of paratroopers, who had been dropped too low. Many of them were touching the earth as their chutes were just popping open, and did not survive impact. It was just terrible to see. There wasn't much time to think about it. We came under fire almost right away.

The air raids were the worst. The fully loaded Japanese planes would swoop right in over us. The pilot would pick out a big ship and dive straight for it. You never knew whether it would be you or not. We were lucky because most of the time we were on smaller ships and were not really the target. Of course, if those pilots had known what we were about, it would have been different. With all the explosives we always had with us, we would have been blown sky high. I always said that if they ever hit us, we would leave a hole in that ocean that would take a week to fill back up.

When the Japanese attacked our shipping convoys, there was nothing we

Landing Ship, Tank or LSTs during WWII were not named. LST-45's International Call Sign was November-Quebec-Charlie-Whiskey (NQCW). Yard Sweeper Mines or YSMs, which were auxiliary motor minesweeper vessels, also were not named.

DAWSON

I especially enjoyed keeping score of the planes we shot down.

DAWSON

Here I am painting the score on the tower.

could really do but go for a gun and hope you could knock the enemy out of the sky before he hit anyone. We shot at them with anything we could get our hands on. It didn't do all that much good, because the Japanese pilots would start their dives pretty high up and out of range. Those big suns painted on their wings sure stood out. We got as many as we could. It was my job to record each successful hit on our ship's tower. It was one of the more satisfying duties I had.

When the Japanese were not trying to kill us, life on board ship was fairly routine. No one knew who we were or what we were doing. Only the top brass knew that, and I don't think all that many of them knew. We frequently transferred from ship to ship and kept to ourselves. The crew would watch us with nervous looks as we carried tons of explosives aboard. They didn't care for that at all.

The twelve landings involving NCDU-2 and NCDU-3 included the first at the Admiralty Islands off the coast of New Guinea previously discussed. The second was a triple-header as they landed at Aitape, Tanahmerah Bay, and Hollandia on 22 April 1944. The Aitape airfield at Tadji was strategic and designated Blue Beach for the invasion. H-hour had been set for 0645 and NCDU-2 and NCDU-3 were in the Special Services Group for pre-assault operations.

Once on board, we stayed together and didn't mix with the other sailors much so we would not have to answer too many questions. We operated under top secret orders and knew the lives of thousands, not to

mention our own lives, depended on keeping our mouths shut.

I remember one time a sailor got into our business. He came up to me and started asking a lot of questions and needling me. He was really an agitator. I can't remember exactly what he said to me, but I do remember he was bothering me. I told him to leave us be, but he just kept it up. It takes a lot of effort to get on my bad side, but this

Name_____ DAWSON, William Louis _____
(Name in Full, Surname to the Left)

256 52 66 _____ Rate_____ GM3c _____
(Service No.)

Date Reported Aboard:_____ 9 September 1943 _____

Naval Combat Demolition Unit No. 2
(Present Ship or Station)

#3 _____ (Ship or Station Received From)

25 May to 6 June 1944:
Participated with credit in the operation at Biak Island, Schouten Group, New Guinea, against Japanese forces.

F.R. Kaine
F.R. Kaine
O-in-C, NCDU #2

#4

30 June to 8 July 1944:
Participated with credit in the operation against Japanese forces at Noemfoor Island, Schouten Group, New Guinea.

F.R. Kaine
F.R. Kaine
O-in-C, NCDU #2

Date Transferred_____

To_____

_____
Signature and Rank of Commanding Officer.

Date Received Aboard:_____

_____
(New Ship or Station)

_____
(Last Ship or Station)

_____
Signature and Rank of Commanding Officer.

ORIGINAL
FOR SERVICE RECORD

guy was persistent. We started to tussle, and I was just plain tired of fooling with him. I ended the fight by picking him up and simply dropping him overboard. He came up spluttering and said that he couldn't swim. I looked over and saw that he was drifting fast toward the stern. It was then that I realized we were under way. I shouted, "Man overboard," and jumped in after him. I swam with him to the stern where someone had dropped over a line. A couple of hours later, the guy stopped by to thank me for saving his life. No one on the ship bothered us after that.

We tried not to talk too much to anyone. The officials never put anything in our records about what we really did. I didn't write home much, because I couldn't say very much about anything.

We often didn't know what we were going to do until we shoved off. Only LTjg Kaine and LTjg Anderson knew what might be about to happen. LTjg Kaine was a good officer. He was tall and thin and could go through the water like a fish. He and Anderson were out there with us for nearly every minute of training, and they were very good at working with the chain of command. Every now and then, they would disappear and then come back with a list of jobs for us. I have no idea where they went or who they talked to, but they always came back with orders.

We slept onboard in bunks overhead and under. The food was edible—better than the dry rations we had in the field. It wasn't always agreeable, but we had to put up with it. We lived next to each other 24 hours a day. I always felt fortunate that the five other guys were such good company. One friend I thought the world of was Sam Pahdopony on NCDU-3. He was a 25-year-old Comanche Indian from Oklahoma. How he learned to swim so well on the prairie, I will never know. I can tell you he was a hell of a good man to have beside you if anything bad was happening.

We spent as much time on deck as possible. I think the other sailors thought we were crazy to lounge around on the rubber hose demolitions, but we spent so much time with explosives that they didn't make us the least bit nervous.

When we had cleared the sand bars at Aitape, we embarked on LSD-181 bound for Cape Cretin in New Guinea. We were to pick up supplies, repair

On top of our explosives was a fine place for us to relax on board ship. No one bothered us there.

Space was tight on LCIs. They didn't have room below for our explosives or us! More often than not, you could find NCDU members relaxing on the TNT.

We kept to ourselves abord ship. We were always transfering from one to another, with scarcely a chance to get to know anyone.

what equipment we could, and then get ready for the next missions.

In May 1944, we got orders to head to the Schouten Islands, part of the Dutch East Indies off the coast of New Guinea. It was going to be a big job, so our units, NCDU-2 and 3, were joined by NCDU-19 and 21. We expected to be clearing ways into the beaches for landings, so we boarded LCI 484 with our usual tons and tons of TNT.

A good day at work looked like this, with explosions that sent water shooting up many feet into the sky.

The commanding officer was a nervous guy. You should have seen his face as we loaded the explosives.

Our first order of business was to conduct surveillance of the islands, named Biak, Noemfoor, and Sansapor. On Biak, we focused on Green Beach at the town of Bosnek. We needed to control the three aerodromes on the east side of the town. Our landing was chaotic. Someone launched rockets too early and then the boats carrying the men got lost in the smoke and haze, driven by strong currents. Somehow, we all got ashore eventually.

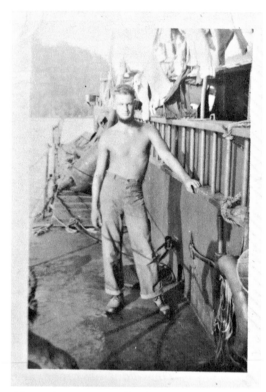

I kept Fort Pierce-fit throughout the war.

We spent May 27 through June 5 blasting channels at Biak. We were under constant attack by Japanese planes. There was nothing you could do, but hope they didn't get you. We worked through two or three air raids a day—and sometimes at night too—with formations of Japanese planes attacking. Some would dive bomb and some would drop bombs. We heard a Japanese task force was headed our way, so we did our best to ignore the bombs falling around us. We worked hard to get ahead of the approaching Japanese.

When we finished the channels at Biak, we went to Noemfoor to blast through the reef there to create

134

three berths for LSTs. We worked under constant Japanese attacks from planes, and also from snipers armed with mortars on the land. When we went ashore to do reconnaissance, we saw lots of dead Japanese and destroyed planes.

After we finally finished there, we got some much-needed rest in Australia, where we stayed from July 27 through August 1. I was able to acquire a roll of color film.

We didn't get to enjoy much of Australia. We were soon ordered back to New Guinea, this time to a village called Gemadodo on Milne Bay. We felt the tide of war was going in our favor. We were slowly pushing the Japanese out of New Guinea, and were weakening their

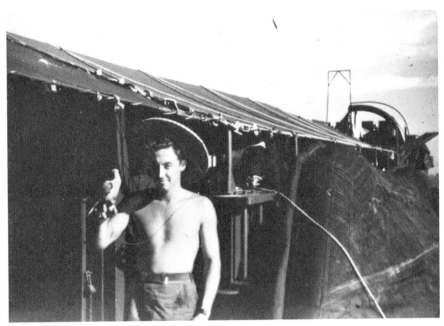

Edward Messall.

Johnny Wilhide.

Color film was a new and rare commodity during the war. I was very excited to find a roll while in Australia. I used it to capture a portrait of every man in NCDU-2 and NCDU-3. We posed near our rubber boat or near the signal flags. We wore our "regular uniform" of shorts and straw hats—not exactly Navy regulation, but it worked for us. I was even able to capture our mascot, a small parrot that moved with our unit from ship to ship.

Cornelius DeVries.

Alar Pierce.

Harrison Eskridge.

James Sandy.

Sam Pahdopony.

Dillard Williams.

LTjg Lloyd Anderson.

LTjg Frank Kaine.

*LTjg Kaine showing off a
captured Japanese flag.*

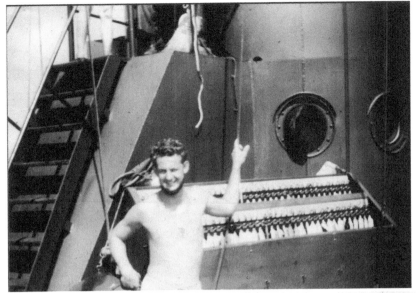

air warfare abilities. The Japanese were losing strategically valuable footholds due, in part, to our work.

When we arrived at Milne Bay, we boarded LCI 228 and got underway on September 26 with some twenty tons of explosives. Two days later, we got hit—not by the Japs, but our own Navy. LCI 340 rammed us and put a really nice hole in our side. We got to work fast and threw on a patch and a brace. The ship that collided with us had no damage. They just rammed us and backed right on out. Our mission was a wash, because even with the patch, we were taking on water fast. We pumped like crazy and returned to Hollandia as fast as we could.

I was able to get up and photograph the damage after we were rammed by LCI 340 in Lingayun Gulf.

Back in port, we met up with some other guys from Class 1, who were in NCDU-24. They were one of the units that participated in the Normandy landings. Those guys had it pretty rough. I remain grateful to this day I was sent to the Pacific. They told us about new units that were training in Hawaii called the Underwater Demolition Teams. The rest of the men of Class 1 who had first been sent Europe were now assigned to these UDTs.

By mid-October, we had a new destination: The Philippines. Our two units were joined by NCDU-20 on an LCI

LCI 228 in August 1944, before she was rammed by LCI 340.

in a giant convoy of ships. It was an incredible force to behold. We knew we were in for something big.

We arrived at the Philippines on October 16 and began reconnaissance work on some of the islands in the Leyte Gulf. We were walking along the beach on the shore of San Pedro Bay just at dawn. It was peaceful, beautiful. We had just finished taking some soundings. The Japs didn't even know we were there.

Apparently the U.S. Army didn't either. Without warning, the shooting started. We hit the sand fast. If I could have dug a hole on the spot, I would have. The first wave of U.S. infantry came right on us, landing and racing up the beach, right past the pillboxes (watch towers) that were still full of Japs.

We had a joke among ourselves. General MacArthur famously said of the Philippines: "I shall return." Well, we got there first!

NCDU-24 had come to join the Pacific NCDUs as the sixth unit in the group and a companion for NCDU-21. NCDU-24 had participated in the Normandy landings, and was the only NCDU that served in both Europe and the Pacific, having not been subsumed into a UDT.

In October 1944, assaults on Yap and Mindanao had been deferred, and the focus became Leyte. On 13 October 1944, NCDUs 2, 3, and 20 left Hollandia in a 130 ship convoy in route to the Philippines.

The Leyte landing was significant, since it included General Douglas MacArthur's return to the Philippines. It was not until the fall of 1944 that General MacArthur and Admiral Nimitz finally planned a joint operation to take back that territory: The invasion of the Philippines, which was the largest sea battle in history, took place in Leyte Gulf.

General MacArthur kept a promise he had made two and a half years earlier to the people of the Philippines; he returned to the islands with an enormous invasion force and the largest assemblage of naval vessels in history.

BNP 608-B
(Revised October 1942)

Corrected Copy

REPORT OF CHANGES

Page

of U.S.S. LCI(L) 227

for the month ending 31st day of July , 19 44 , date of sailing

from to

	NAMES (Alphabetically arranged without regard to ratings, with surname to the left and the first name written in full)	SERVICE NUMBER (The service number must under no condition be omitted)	Rating at Date of Last Report	Date of Enlistment		Place of Enlistment
		2	3	4		5
1	ARMSTRONG, William J.	882 96 10	M1c			
2	DAWSON, William L.	256 62 66	GM3c			
3	DEVRIES, Cornelius C.	562 79 46	AOM1c			
4	ESKRIDGE, Harrison Q.	829 86 22	GM3c			
5	MESSALL, Edward A.	671 50 94	GM3c			
6	PAHDOPONY, Sam (n)	671 50 76	GM3c			
7	PIERCE, Eler H.	837 45 49	MM1c			
8	SANDY, James D.	834 99 20	GM3c			
9	WILHIDE, John N. Jr.	829 80 79	GM3c			
10	WILLIAMS, Dillard E.	829 89 10	GM3c			
11	FRENCH, Aubrey A.	258 46 01	MoMM2c			
12						
13						
14						
15						

	Branch of service 6	Received, transferred, deserted, discharged, change of rating, death, or any other change of status 7	Date of occurrence in column 7 8	Vessel or station from which received, to what vessel or station transferred, where discharged and character of discharge; where deserted, and amount due or overpaid. Where died, cause of death and where and when buried. If raied and authority for same. If deserted, give cause; if on detached duty, give place of duty. If passenger, give purpose of travel and final disposition. 9
1	USN-I	TRANS.	18 July 1944	Transferred to USS LCI(L) 228 Auth: Verbal Orders Commander Day.
2	USN	"	"	" " " " "
3	USNR	"	"	" " " " "
4	USNR	"	"	" " " " "
5	USNR	"	"	" " " " "
6	USNR	"	"	" " " " "
7	USNR	"	"	" " " " "
8	USN-I	"	"	" " " " "
9	USNR-SV	"	"	" " " " "
10	USNR-SV	"	"	" " " " "
11	USN	"	31 July 1944	Transferred to ComServForLant. Auth: BuPers Despatch 201230 of Dec. 1943.
12				
13				
14				
15				

This form to be submitted by commanding officers of all ships and stations, whenever any ship or station is commissioned or placed out of commission, on the last day of each month showing all changes for the month for which submitted; also upon sailing from one port to another, by commanding officers of point of origin of transfer and point of destination of enlisted passengers.

A typical NCDU muster list from an LCI--we were leaving Milne Bay en route to Australia.

141

1944   DAWSON

A brief moment of peace on deck between operations.

COMMENDATION

On 19 August 1944 this man received a letter of commendation from Commander Seventh Amphibous Force for work done on 2 July 1944 at Noemfoor Island, Dutch New Guinea

Copy of letter is enclosed in this man's jacket.

J.C. Sibigtroth
Lt. USNR
Commanding

Date Transferred _____

To _____

_____
Signature and Rank of Commanding Officer.

Date Received Aboard: _____

_____
(New Ship or Station)

_____
(Last Ship or Station)

_____
Signature and Rank of Commanding Officer.

ORIGINAL

1944   WILLIAMS   PAHDOPONY   DAWSON

We are gathered in a gun tub, or what we called gun emplacements, on an LCI tied up some place.

After the excitement, we went to work. We had our hands full getting rid of booby traps, disarming mines, and disposing of unexploded ordnance. We also blasted room for the PBYs, seaplane patrol bombers, which were used for reconnaissance.

Being part of a big convoy meant we were also a big target. The Jap planes came at us really low, practically skimming the water. They would jump over us, then skim the water again, gunning for their targets: The bigger ships in our battle group. They flew low to make it harder for us to shoot them down, and, when they hit their targets, they made a hole in the side of the ship at the water line, making it more likely they would sink or cripple any vessel they could hit. The assaults were constant, one right after another, and we lived in a state of high alert. On October 24, my log recorded two LCIs hit, one sunk, as well as a tug sunk. We shot down 29 Jap planes, and I think our guys personally got one. Another day, a liberty cargo ship got hit by a dive-bombing Jap plane. Our forces across the convoy shot down at least 200 Jap planes that day.

The air attacks continued without relief every day from dawn on into the night. We were harder to hit at night because we kept all lights off. Our only relief was almost as bad as the attacks themselves. On October 29, we were hit by a typhoon just before midnight.

An LCI in a typhoon is a wild, wild ride. It was like being in hell. I am not the type to get seasick, but a lot of guys were. You could not stand up, and if you tried to move around, you got thrown about pretty bad. The only thing you could do was brace yourself in your bunk. Sleeping was impossible. If you weren't scared, there was something wrong with you. That ship went every which way but the right way. At least we took comfort that as long as we were being heaved this way and that; we hadn't yet run aground or hit coral. As bad as we were being tossed, it was better than sinking.

When the typhoon cleared, our convoy was spread out all over the Pacific. That didn't stop the Japs. They came at us again as soon as they could get back in the air. This time, there wasn't even a break at night. Our relief again came in the form of another typhoon. Typhoons don't get any easier the second time around. The Japs hit us harder than ever when the second typhoon cleared. Seven ships got hit.

The Battle of Leyte Gulf officially started on October 23 and ended October 26, but for those of us

General MacArthur talking to the troops after wading ashore at Leyte.

General MacArthur walking along our invasion route from the San Pedro Bay inland.

Loading torpedos.

143

Name **DAWSON, William Louis**
(Name in Full, Surname to the Left)

256-52-66 Rate **GM2c**
(Service No.)

Date Reported Aboard: **28 August 1944**

USS LCI (L) 228 NCDU #2
(Present Ship or Station)

RB Navy 167
(Ship or Station Received From)

#5

Participated in the initial
landing on Leyte Island,
Philippines, on October 20, 194
Acquitted himself admirably on
many occasions under fire of
enemy planes.

J. C. Sibigtroth
Lt. (jg) USNR
Commanding.

Date Transferred

To

Signature and Rank of Commanding Officer.

Date Received Aboard:

(New Ship or Station)

(Last Ship or Station)

Signature and Rank of Commanding Officer.

ORIGINAL
FOR SERVICE RECORD

in it, the attacks lasted without let-up through the middle of November.

We moved on to Mindoro, another island in the Philippines and then to Thckloban, a city on the Leyte Gulf. That is where we spent Christmas. It didn't feel like a holiday. I got a couple of letters from home, which was nice. We didn't get much mail, so a letter was always special. We didn't write much because we couldn't say much. The officers bought us some beer and some of the guys made decorations for our berths on the ship. There were air raids all night, but Christmas Day itself was quiet.

We were in transit to the Lingayen Gulf when a kamikaze crashed into an escort aircraft carrier in our convoy. The ship was filled with ordinance, which made for a huge and violent fire. The order was given to abandon ship before the whole thing blew. We did our best to help and rescued some of the sailors.

NCDU #2+3 1944

Loading bangalore torpedos, which are five feet long, cross-wise on our rubber boat.

Next up for us was what became known as the Battle of Lingayen Gulf. We didn't know what we were in for yet. We just knew that before the 6th Army began their assault, we had to begin ours. We didn't encounter too many problems, and the work was especially satisfying. Lingayen was where General MacArthur was pushed out of the Philippines back in 1941, and now three years later, we were coming back. I had great pictures of General MacArthur, but they got away from me over the years.

On board an LCI after another successful operation— we are wearing the straw hats that we bartered to get.

We had some time to explore the abandoned Japanese defenses. They had some frightfully big guns, now silent and in our control. After the pounding we had taken since October from all the air raids and the typhoons, it was satisfying to walk through these strongholds knowing we won.

The landings were just a start. We had more winning to do in the Philippines. By the end of February, we were attacking Palawan. The idea was to expand the Allied range of operations. From Palawan, we could reach as far as Indochina and deny the Japanese access to the South China Sea. We could also cut off Japanese oil supplies from Borneo.

We spent the months of March and April 1945 in a blur of operations. In Zamboanga we cleared mines on the shore and along the dock areas. We worked in darkness to be ready for the bombardment that started at 6:45 in the morning. Before the Battle of Cebu City on March 26, we did the same thing. The beaches were heavily mined, so we had to work all morning, even through the initial bombardment that began at 7:00 in the morning and through

The NCDU-2 and NCDU-3 men began the New Year aboard the *USS Clemson* (APD-31) in route for the invasion of Lingayen Gulf. There were many ships in the group, and about twenty of them were hit with Kamikaze planes on the way to Lingayen.

One of the ships sunk was the escort aircraft carrier *USS Ommaney Bay* (CVE-79), when, on 2 January 1945, a twin-engine Japanese suicide plane penetrated the screen undetected and nicked the island-bridge of the ship then crashed into her starboard side. Two bombs were released; one penetrated the flight deck and detonated below, setting off a series of explosions among the fully-fueled planes on the forward third of the hangar deck. The second bomb passed through the hangar deck, ruptured the fire main on the second deck, and exploded near the starboard side.

The order to abandon ship was given. A total of 95 Navy men were lost, including two killed aboard an assisting destroyer, when torpedo warheads on the carrier's hangar deck finally went off. After rescuing the men, a U.S. destroyer sank the the doomed carrier with torpedoes.

The captain of this liberty ship bought a quart of beer for every NCDU man aboard. And one fellow seems to have acquired an entire barrel full.

Name DAWSON, William Louis
(Name in Full, Surname to the Left).

256 52 66 Rate GM2c
(Service No.)

Date Reported Aboard: 28 August 1944

USS LCI (L) 228 NCDU #2
(Present Ship or Station)

RB Navy 167
(Ship or Station Received From)

#6

Subject man participated in the
invasion of Mindoro, P. I., 15th
December 1944 and acquitted himsel
with coolness and courage during
several attacks by enemy planes.

J. C. Sibigtroth
Lt. USNR

Date Transferred_____

To_____

Signature and Rank of Commanding Officer.

Date Received Aboard:_____

(New Ship or Station)

(Last Ship or Station)

Signature and Rank of Commanding Officer.

ORIGINAL
FOR SERVICE RECORD

We found that the straw hats that we traded with the the natives to get worked great in the field. In the back is Sam Pahdopony with Ed Messall, Harrison Eskridge, and Lloyd Anderson. I am left holding the flag with Alar Pierce on the right.

Combat operations for the NCDU men at Lingayen Gulf began at D minus 16 on 9 January 1945 (i.e., 16 hours before the assault was to begin), again with the pre-bombardment group, where they performed a variety of pre-assault reconnaissance and demolition tasks.

The Invasion of Lingayen Gulf was an Allied amphibious operation in the Philippines involving U.S. Navy and Royal Australian Navy warships, which began bombarding suspected Japanese positions along the coast from their positions out in the Lingayen Gulf on 6 January. NCDU operations began the next day on 7 January with covering air and naval gunfire. By the time Bill and his teammates got ashore, they found no beach obstacles and encountered sparse opposing forces.

On 9 January, the U.S. Army landed on a 20-mile beachhead between the towns of Lingayen and San Fabian.

the first troops hitting the beach an hour and a half later.

Everywhere we went, we saw destruction. Boats were burnt and washed up on the shore. Planes were crashed and bent. Buildings were in ruins. I was so struck by the waste of it all. Here we were in paradise,

Name DAWSON, William Louis
(Name in full, surname to the left)

256 52 66   rate   GM2c
(Service number)

Date reported aboard 28 August 1944

NCDU # 2   USS LCI (D) 228
(Present ship or station)

RB Navy 167
(Ship or station received from)

#7

This man participated in the Linga
Gulf, Luzon, Philippine Islands
operation on 6 January 1945, D-3 d
He acquitted himself with coolness
and courage during many attacks by
enemy planes.

F. R. Kaine
F. R. Kaine
O-in-C, NCDU

Date transferred _____

To _____

Signature and rank of Commanding Officer.

Date received aboard _____

(New ship or station)

(Last ship or station)

Signature and rank of Commanding Officer.

ORIGINAL

FOR SERVICE RECORD

16—22321-

Name DAWSON, William Louis
256 52 66   Rate   GM2c

Date reported aboard   28 AUGUST 1944

USS LCI (D) 228 NCDU #2

RB Navy 167
ship or station received from

#8

Subject man participated with credit
inital landing on 10, March, 1945 on
Zamboanga Peninsula, Mindanoa. P.I.

R. M. Kearns
R.M. Kearns
Lt (jg) USNR

Transferred_____
TO_____

signature and rank of c.c

Received aboard_____

new ship or station

last ship or station

signature and rank of C.O.

NAME   DAWSON, William Louis

256 52 66 Rate   GM2c

Date Reported Aboard   28 August 1944

USS LCI (D) 228   NCDU #2
Present Ship or Station

RB Navy 167
Ship or Station Received From

#9   7 April 1945

This man took part in the initial landings at Talisay, Cebu, P.I. on 26 March
1945. He exhibited coolness and courage
while under enemy fire during this landing.

R. M. Kearns
R. M. Kearns
Lt. (jg) USNR
Commanding.

147

I am posing here with one of the ship's crew who came ashore with us.

These were not Japanese guns. They were installed before the war to protect the Philippines, but were never fired. Back row: Me, with Sam Pahdopony, a fellow from the ship's crew, and Dillard Williams. At the front is Harrison Eskridge, Alar Pierce, and another member of the ship's crew.

Me with one of the ship's crew on one of the Filipino guns.

in truly beautiful places, and everywhere there was wreckage.

The Filipinos were grateful to be finally free of the Japanese and treated us very well. They were eager to trade with us. We bartered for some straw hats that did a good job protecting us from the sun. In the pictures I took during this time, we sure didn't look like regular Navy. After so long eating shipboard fare from cans and powder, it sure was nice to get fresh fruit like bananas and pineapples.

On April 17, we were in Polloc Harbor, expecting another pre-dawn operation of clearing mines and removing booby traps. We didn't find any, so the invasion went ahead more or less without us. It was the day after that when I had a moment to think. It was April 18, 1945, my birthday. It had been nearly two years since I enlisted in the Navy.

A crashed Japanese zero fighter plane like those that attacked our ships.

A wrecked Japanese barge.

149

NAME DAWSON, William Louis

256 52 66   Rate   GM2c
Service No.

Date Received Aboard 28 August 1944

     USS LCI (D) 228   NCDU #2
     Present Ship or Station

          RB Navy 167
     Ship or Station Received From

     #10

This man participated in the initial
Malabang - Parang - Cotabato, Mindanao
P.I. landing operations on April 17
1945 against Japanese forces.

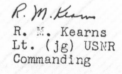

               R. M. Kearns
               R. M. Kearns
               Lt. (jg) USNR
               Commanding

Date Transferred_____

TO_____

_____

Date Received Aboard_____

We spent most of our time on LCIs like this one. These ships were very cramped. They had ramps on each side that they would lower when they hit the beach during an invasion. Soldiers would run down each side and fight their way ashore. We used those ramps to store our explosives.

This native in a dugout canoe showed us the head of a Japanese soldier. He wasn't trying to trade it; he was just showing us that he was on our side.

Wrecked Japanese barges run aground.

One of our wrecked PBY planes.

CONFIDENTIAL

ACTION REPORT

ORIGINAL

USS LCI (D) 228

SERIAL - NONE 5 APRIL 1945

ACTION REPORT - INVASION OF CEBU, P.I.

COVERS ACTIVITY AS DEMOLITION SHIP FOR LANDINGS AT TALISAY POINT SOUTHWEST OF CEBU CITY, FROM 26 MARCH TO 4 APRIL 1945.

132697

OFFICE OF NAVAL RECORDS AND LIBRARY

FF-9148

USS LCI (D) 228
% Fleet Post Office
San Francisco, Calif.

A16-3

5 April 1945

Confidential

From: Commanding Officer
To: Commander-in-Chief, U. S. Fleet

Via: Commander Task Group 78.2
            Commander Task Force 78
            Commander Seventh Fleet

Subject: Action Report - Invasion of Cebu, P.I.

Reference: (a) Com7thPhib Conf. ltr. FE25/A16-3(3) serial
            0212 dated 17 Feb. 1945
            (b) ConinCh restr. ltr. FF1/A12-1/A16-3(3)
            serial 7152 of 29 October 1943

Enclosure: (A) Report by NCDUs #2 and #3
            (B) Report of AA action

    1.   This ship got underway at 1835, 24 March 1945 in convoy with other amphibious craft to take part in the landing at Talisay, Cebu, P. I.

    2.   On E-day this ship went to general quarters at 0642. Approached Green beach III at 0916 on orders of Beach Master to enable demolition units to begin work; Enclosure A details work accomplished. Remained at anchorage until ship joined retirement group at 1620 upon notification of submarine contact. Returned at anchorage at 0750, 27 March 1945.

    3.   At 1925, 27 March, 1945 went to General Quarters upon sighting one enemy plane. Enclosure (B) gives details of this action.

    4.   On 29 March 1945 at 1105 this ship moored portside to dock at Cebu City in order to carry out demolition work in adjacent waters. This ship was the first United States ship to moor at these docks of this task group.

    5.   Upon completion of demolition work and by orders of Commander Task Unit 78.2.3 joined returning echelon on 4 April at 0830.

R. M. Kearns
R.M.Kearns
Lt. (jg) USNR

Advance copy to
  Cominch US Fleet
Copies to:
  Com LCI(G) Gr 20
  Com LCS Flot 1
  Com LCI (L) Flot 15

FILMED   8 01109

132697

CONFIDENTIAL

ACTION REPORT

ORIGINAL

COMMANDER TASK UNIT 78.1.3

SERIAL - NONE 3 MAY 1945

ACTION REPORTS, VESSELS OF TASK UNIT 78.1.3, TARAKAN OPERATION, APRIL 28 - MAY 2, 1945.

[IMPORTANT COMPOSITE REPORT FOR TARAKAN OPERATION.]

133275

OFFICE OF NAVAL RECORDS AND LIBRARY

USS LCI (D) 228
% Fleet Post Office
San Francisco, Calif.

CONFIDENTIAL   1 May 1945

From: Commanding Officer
To: Commander in Chief, U.S. Fleet

Via: Commander Task Unit 78.1.3
               Commander Task Group 78.1
               Commander Seventh Amphibious Force
               Commander Seventh Fleet

Subject: Action Report, Invasion of Tarakan Island, Borneo.

Reference: (a) Com7thPhib conf. ltr. FE25/A16-3(3)
               serial 0212 dated 17 Feb. 45

Enclosure: Report by NCDUs #2 and 3. - p.31

        1.   This ship got underway at 0930, 25 April 1945
with minesweeping unit, Commander Task Unit 78.1.5, to take
part in landing at Tarakan Island, Borneo.

        2.   At 0822, 26 April 1945, on orders from Commander
Task Unit 78.1.5, this ship along with USS LCI (M) 359, left
formation to investigate rafts with Japanese personnel aboard.
Upon closing raft commanding officer called to occupants and
attempted to take occupants prisoners. Occupants made no effort
to surrender and immediately began adjusting some object about
their waists. This ship opened fire, with automatic weapons,
and destroyed raft and five Japanese aboard raft. As first
shots struck raft a small explosion was seen to occur on raft.

        3. On P-four day this ship arrived in area off
Tarakan Island, Borneo and stood by to assist in minesweeping
and demolition work as required. No demolition was carried
out by this vessel. Retired on P-four, P-three, P-two and P-one
day in accordance with Annex "L" of Oboe-operation plan.

        4.   On P-day this ship anchored in assigned area near
Lingkas beach, Tarakan Island, Borneo and stood by for orders
to do demolition work. See Enclosure A.

                                R. M. Kearns
                                R. M. Kearns
                                Lt. (jg) USNR

Advance Copy to:
  Cominch, U.S.Fleet
Copies to:
  ComLCSFlot One
  ComLCI(R) Gr.20
  CTU 78.1.5

38   35

CONFIDENTIAL

ACTION REPORT

COMMANDER TASK UNIT 78.1.3

SERIAL - NONE   3 MAY 1945

ACTION REPORTS, VESSELS OF TASK UNIT 78.1.3, TARAKAN
OPERATION, APRIL 28 - MAY 2, 1945.

[IMPORTANT COMPOSITE REPORT FOR
TARAKAN OPERATION.]

133275

USS LCI (D) 228
℅ Fleet Post Office
San Francisco, Calif.

4 April 1945

From: Officers-in-Charge of NCDU 2 and 3.
To: Commander Seventh Amphibious Force.

Via: Commanding Officer - USS LCI (D) 228

Subject: Report of Operations, 26 March 1945 to 3 April
            1945 with Victor-Two Attach Group.

Reference: Operation Plan No. 3-45

1.   Upon arrival at the objective area, this unit
reported to the Beachmaster as directed. The unit was ordered
to investigate and remove the landing craft barricades that
were placed offshore on and to the right of Green Beach Three.
These barricades were removed by towing them out of the beaching
area and securing them on the reef to the north-east of the
Breen Beaches. The barricades were in the form of hard timber
and coconut logs, bamboo, small boats, and any other floating
material that could be lashed together to form the obstruction.
All of the material was lashed together with wire cable, strung
out along the shore about 60 yards off the beach, and anchored
in place. The only operation necessary was to cut the cables
that anchored the obstruction and tow the entire line out of
the way. Those parts that were not attached to the main line
were then removed singly. It was not necessary to remove the
barbed wire and anti-boat stakes, that were on the water's edge
as they were placed to the right of the beaches we used.

2.   On D plus 2, our divers were ordered to report
to the ATA 179 to assist in clearing an anchor cable from the
screws of that vessel. However, other divers from the Spencer
were already clearing the screws so the assistance of this
unit was not needed.

3.   On D plus # the unit assisted in a reconnaissance
of the dock area in the city. It was necessary to dive on some
sunken barges, in what was to become the LST landing beach, to
see if they could be removed with the use of explosives. It
was possible to 'eliminate' them so the explosives were laid and
the barges blow up. The largest piece that was left and could
be found, was then towed up on shore and used in the fill-in.

8 91109

4.   Starting on D plus 4 the unit was at work on clearing out a section of the Dock that had been hit by an aerial bomb. It was necessary to cut down a one-half inch steel retaining wall, and clear out the piling and rails that were in the way. The approach was to be cleared so an LSM or an LST could 'Beach' for unloading in the cleared shpace. The area was successfully cleared and ready for use when the ships arrived although the work was slightly hampered by the arrival of a liberty ship that was docked near-by.

5.   The unit's divers also went down to inspect a 110' foot Japanese barge that was sunken along one section of the dock. It was found to be an open hatch barge and there was no possibility of closing the hatches nor of pumping it out. It was too close to the dock installations to permit blowing it out of the way. Proper report was made to the Beachmaster.

6.   The unit's divers also went down and attached cables to a 105 mm Anti-Tank Destroyer that had dropped to the bottom when the hositing cables had parted on the liberty ship. The diving was done in approximately 32 to 35 feet of water.

7.   Inspection was made of some Japanese torpedos that were in the dock and fort area, to determine if they could be safely shipped out. The inspection was made for SOPA (CTG 78.2.3) and verbal report was given him. No action was taken by the officers of this unit, as the torpedos were of an unfamiliar type.

8.   A reconnaisance was made of the area along the seawall between piers 2 and 3 in an effort to locate a sunken Japanese submarine that was reportedly in that area. Divers went down in shallow water rigs and grapnels were used from h the surface but the submarine could not be located.

9.   No casualties were suffered in either unit during the operation although some enemy shells landed nearby while the units were in the water removing the log barricades.

10.   One of the unit's 10 man reubber boats was damaged beyond repair during the operation and should be replaced.

L. G. Anderson
O-in-C NCDU #3

F. F. Kaine
O-in-C- NCDU #2

Copy:to:
   CTG 78.2

8 01103

158

Americans bring light   *Morning Times*   *Freedom is dawning*

Published by instructions of Cebu Area Command (USFIP)

Vol. 2 — Saturday, 31 March 1945 — No. 16

SOLOMONS VETERANS LIBERATE CEBU CITY

* * * * * * * * * *

JAPANESE RETREAT AS AMERICANS ADVANCE

LANDING OPERATIONS CARRIED OUT UNDER COVER OF HEAVY AERIAL AND NAVAL BOMBARDMENTS. ENEMY CAUGHT OFF GUARD. OFFERS MODERATE RESISTANCE

At all times the Filipino people will always look upon President Franklin D. Roosevelt of the United States as their great liberator and benefactor. To him they are ever grateful for making the Philippines a pattern of civilization in the Orient.

Under cover of heavy naval and aerial bombardments, the Americans landed at Talisay, 5 miles southwest of Cebu City on Monday morning. Preliminary to the landing, enemy positions along the coast were softened up by aerial and naval bombardments.

The landing announced by Gen. MacArthur's Wednesday communique drives a wedge between Negros and Bohol, the only remaining big islands still in Japanese hands.

Americal Division Lands

The Japanese were caught off guard and offered only moderate resistance. When the "Water Buffalos" landed the Japanese opened fire with trench mortars and 19-mm guns, but later on were spotted by American planes and silenced.

The Americans that effected the landing, veterans of the Solomons campaign, were under Major General William Arnold. They comprised the Americal Division of the 8th U.S. Army.

Continue on page 4

Pass this to a friend.

Ryukyu Islands Under Bombardment

The Ryukyus, a group of islands northeast of Formosa and 300 miles south of the Japanese mainland, has been subjected to heavy bombardment by American carrier aircraft and battleships since Friday, March 23. Good results were reported by Guam.

It was also reported that Marianas-based superfortresses bombed the Omura airplane plant on Kyushu and the military installations of Pachiari and Orita.

Japs In Mindanao Suffering From Malaria

Although suffering from malaria, the Japanese in Mindanao are desperately resisting the advancing American forces, according to Radio Tokyo.

15,024 Japanese Killed On Luzon In 10 Days

General Douglas MacArthur reported that the American forces in the first ten days on Luzon killed or captured 15,024 Japanese. Enemy losses in the Luzon campaign now total more than 297,000.

Anti-German Demonstration Spreading In German Cities

Anti-Nazi demonstrations are spreading in many scuttled German cities as the allied offensive east of the Rhine enters its decisive phase, Stockholm report stated. German civilians are no longer heeding Hitler.

Landing In Cebu . . .

(Continued from page 1)

March 28 (Special to Morning Times) The Japanese in Cebu City area are facing complete destruction as the advancing 8th Army troops from their landing point at Talisay, and the Filipino guerrilla forces from the mountains push forward, catching the enemy within the tightening ring of encirclement.

Earlier report indicates that the advancing American and Filipino troops are converging into the heart of the city proper. Heavy fighting is raging in the outskirts of the city.

Field dispatches disclose that the Filipino troops from the mountains are breaking through the enemy's outer defenses. The enemy, being attacked from the rear, is desperately resisting, wantonly destroying private property as he retreats.

(Continue on page 6)

Germans Surrender To American Pilot

A good number of German soldiers rushed to surrender themselves to an American pilot who bailed out from his damaged plane and landed on enemy territory. The Germans thought that paratroopers were going to land.

Japanese Planes Attempt To Raid U.S. Task Force

A small group of Japanese planes attempted to raid the U.S. task force that bombarded Okinawa. Six of the enemy planes were destroyed.

MANILA FALL OPENS NEW WAR PHASE

"Japan itself is our final goal. . . Our motto becomes: 'On to Tokyo.'"

In these ringing words General MacArthur in Manila on Tuesday emphasized to the world that the fall of Manila, great as that victory is, is but a stage in the defeat of Japan.

Following is General MacArthur's brief statement, made as the last surrounded Jap defenders in Manila faced the certainty of destruction:

"The fall of Manila marks the end of one great phase of the Pacific struggle and sets the stage for another. We shall not rest until our enemy is completely overthrown. We do not count anything done as long as anything remains to be done. We are well on the way, but Japan itself is our final goal.

"With Australia saved, the Philippines liberated and the ultimate redemption of the East Indies and Malaya thereby made a certainty, our motto becomes: 'On to Tokyo.'

"We are ready in this veteran and proven command when called upon.

"May God speed the day."

Japan's Oil Supply Hit

British East Indies naval forces have carried out their most damaging blow to date on Japanese oil supplies in a series of attacks on southern Sumatra, a special communique from Allied headquarters reported last week.

This new assault on Japan's sources of oil adds to damage done, previously by MacArthur's bombers on Borneo.

Carrier-borne planes attacked the refinery at Palembang on January 29th, the communique said. The Japanese defended their oil installations with fighter aircraft from several fields. Sixty-five Jap planes were destroyed during the series of blows, 27 of them in air combat and the remainder on the ground.

In addition to aircraft carriers, the ships participating in the action included the battleship, King George V, the warships, Argonaut, Black Prince, Euralus, Grenville, Kempenfelt and Uras. None of the ships were damaged in the operations. Fifteen planes were lost.

MESSAGE FROM FDR RECEIVED BY OSMENA

Washington, Feb. 7—President Roosevelt hailed the liberation of Manila in a message to President Osmena. The President said:

"Let the enemies of peaceful nations take warning from these great events in your country. Their world of treachery, aggression and enslavement cannot survive in the struggle against our world of freedom and peace."

U. S. Strongly Supports P. I. Freedom, Says Romulo

The people of the United States are intensely interested in the cause of Philippine freedom, Brig. Gen. Carlos P. Romulo, resident commissioner of the Philippines in the United States, said Sunday in Tacloban, enroute to General MacArthur's Luzon headquarters.

General Romulo accompanied President Osmena and other Commonwealth officials into Manila with General MacArthur when the Philippines capital was liberated.

Romulo returned from the United States with President Osmena Saturday. He spoke twice on the floor of Congress, wrote a number of articles for leading magazines and newspapers and was a leading speaker on the radio program, "We, the People" and other top radio shows.

During his visit he made an extended speaking tour through the United States and told the American people of the historic role played by Filipino resistance in defeating the Japs.

He declared that his trip had been a great success and that everywhere he went he found the Americans enthusiastic. His speeches in Congress were received with acclaim and one was given a spontaneous standing ovation.

Leyte-Samar FREE PHILIPPINES

PUBLISHED TWICE A WEEK

VOL. I   Tacloban, Leyte, Thursday February 8, 1945   13—16—F8   No. 28.

Voice of Freedom
5—5:30 p.m. 7.795 Mc.
Philippine Hour
9—9:15 a.m. 15.5 Mc.
6—7 p.m. 9.615 Mc.

Manila's Liberation Nears; Japs Doomed

MacArthur Confers With Aides

Osmena Enters Capital With Victorious Forces

President Osmena arrived at General MacArthur's headquarters in Luzon Sunday to enter Manila with Gen. MacArthur.

The President was accompanied by Brigadier General Carlos P. Romulo, resident commissioner of the Philippines in the United States, and other Commonwealth officials.

Osmena flew directly to MacArthur's Luzon headquarters from Tacloban Sunday, following his return from the United States where he has been conferring with high officials on immediate problems of relief and rehabilitation for the Filipino people.

President Osmena said that his conferences in Washington on relief needs for the Philippines were a success and that he will return to Washington for conferences with President Roosevelt as soon as basic problems in the restoration of the Philippine Commonwealth Government are solved.

Soviets Roll Nearer Berlin

The Battle of Berlin rolled nearer the showdown stage as the great Russian offensive pounded from three directions toward the German capital. More than a hundred villages were captured in the latest Russian advances as a mounting state of chaos gripped Berlin. Zhukov's First White Russian Army drove from the northeast, east and southeast on a broad front as the German people were bluntly told that the enemy was ready to launch a frontal attack on the capital.

Powerful Russian forces have outflanked Kustrin, German Oder River stronghold, and captured Barwalde, 38 miles from Berlin. Other units of the White Russian Army, indicating a flanking movement on the southern end of the line, captured Ziebigen, 13 miles southeast of Frankfort on the Oder.

Directly aiding the Russians, the U. S. Fourth Airforce sent 1000 "Forts" over Berlin, scoring eight direct hits on German government buildings including the War Office.

U. S. FORCES FREE 5000 INTERNEES

G. H. Q., Southwest Pacific Area, Feb. 7—American forces during the week were completing final stages of the liberation of Manila after victorious columns of three of General MacArthur's forces had simultaneously entered the capital from the east, north and south and completely surrounded the last Japanese defenders of the city.

General MacArthur reported that the Japanese in Manila face "complete destruction."

The liberation of the first great capital of the Far East to be wrested from control of the Japanese oppressors was marked by the dramatic rescue of approximately 5000 civilian internees, 4000 of them American, from Santo Tomas and Bilibid concentration camps. Women and children were included among the rescued internees from the two camps.

First Cavalry Leads Way

Advance elements of the First Cavalry who freed the Santo Tomas prisoners were the first of MacArthur's forces to enter Manila Saturday night, sweeping down from the north in a wide enveloping arc. Shortly afterward, elements of the 37th Infantry drove into the city to capture Bilibid prison and rescue 800 prisoners of war and 550 civilian internees. 3700 were rescued from Santo Tomas.

Simultaneous entrance in force into Manila was made Sunday by columns of the First Cavalry, the 37th Infantry and the 11th Airborne division, which swept into the city after a lightning overnight thrust of 35 miles from Tagaytay, seized by the 11th in parachute landings the day before.

West of Manila, MacArthur's forces bottled up Bataan, gaining complete control of all roads leading into the peninsula after a junction of 11th corps elements with those of the 14th.

San Jose Taken

In the northeastern sector of the Luzon central plains, forces of the First Corps captured San Jose and cut the road to Baleta and the Cagayan valley.

Heavy bombers operating in the China sea pounded the Japanese air base at Okayama Sunday, destroying 20 parked planes and starting many fires and explosions. Patrol planes destroyed or damaged four small freighters in a series of attacks along the Formosa coast and in the Sakishima Islands.

Superforts Hit Kobe

Superfortresses from bases in the Marianas hit the Kobe industrial area of Japan another smashing blow last week without losing a plane to enemy action.

Forty-two Jap planes were destroyed or damaged in the operation. Good bombing results were reported.

Filipino Patriots

American troops have landed in your area. They come to liberate you from the Japanese.

TO HELP DEFEAT THE JAPS, AND FOR YOUR OWN SAFETY:

STAY AWAY FROM MILITARY OBJECTIVES, wherever there are Jap soldiers or installations.

AVOID ROADS AND BRIDGES. They will be bombed and strafed.

Remember--We do not want to harm YOU, but bombs cannot tell friend from foe. So do not gather in large groups.

If the Japs compel you to remain in dangerous areas, build slit trenches for yourselves.

Do not wander around at night. Our patrols will shoot at any moving figure.

KEEP CALM. DO NOT ACT HASTILY AND EXPOSE YOUR-SELF UNNECESSARILY TO ENEMY REPRISALS.

REMAIN READY TO HELP US WHEN THE OPPORTUNITY COMES

If you find Allied soldiers who have been separated from their units, hide them safely from the Japs, and notify the nearest American Headquarters.

If they are wounded give them as much medical care as you can.

FOLLOW THESE INSTRUCTIONS and help us drive the Japs from your island!

7J6

We were supplied with flyers that we could hand out to people we met. They were designed to let Filipinos know that we were liberators, not invaders. The people we met didn't need flyers to know that we were the good guys. They were happy to see us.

Chapter 8
To Borneo and Victory

On April 25, 1945, we got underway for Tarakan in Borneo, which we were told was a small marshy piece of land off North Kalimantan, Indonesia in the eastern Celebes Sea.

We had an interesting encounter along the way. Someone on our LCI spotted a group of people on a raft. It was hard to see them. They were waving their hands, and we thought at first that they were survivors from a shipwreck. When we got closer, we could see they had white heads. They were shouting to us in English, "Come closer, come closer."

We told the commanding officer to be careful. We had seen a lot in our two years of war. When you see something curious, be cautious. When we got closer, we could see that their heads were shaved—not that their heads were white. Some of us thought they looked like Japanese. What would a bunch of people with shaved heads be doing on a raft way out here?

We warned the commanding officer of our LCI, and suggested if the people on the raft wanted something from us, they should swim over to us. Our LCI commander was a young lieutenant junior grade and he did not share our sense of caution. He maneuvered the ship to get closer to them.

That is when the bald men on the raft opened up. They stood and began lobbing hand grenades at us. That cured the curiosity of our commanding officer! He backed the engines and opened fire on them with our 40-millimeter gun. That first burst of bullets from us hit the raft, which exploded in a

The men of the demonstration invasion watch one of our charges go off, You can see the wooden stakes driven into the sand that could easily puncture the bottom of landing vessels.

164

huge geyser of water. It turns out the raft had been loaded with depth charges.

That was our first, but not last encounter with suicide rafts. We ran into a bunch more. We sank two and our planes got another six that day.

Later in the afternoon, we got our orders to clear the obstacles at Tarakan. NCDU-2 and 3 worked together with NCDU-20 and 24. We didn't know it, but it was our last operation. Led by the Australians, and assisted by the Dutch, our job was a demonstration bombardment and amphibious assault. A "demonstration" was meant to distract and confuse the enemy while the real attack happened somewhere else. We began our recon on April 27, but didn't begin clearing obstacles until the day before the planned demonstration assault.

Under a heavy smoke screen, NCDU-20 and 24 began work at 11:00 on April 30. They teamed with Australian engineers to clear rows of wooden stakes, wire, and iron obstacles. These obstacles were the first we had encountered in the Pacific. The men that landed at Normandy had more experience with these kinds of beach obstructions, so they were the first to go in. My units NCDU-2 and NCDU-3 were on stand-by, but got the call after the troops landed around 7:30 on May 1. We went in around 9:00 and took out three rows of pilings, log floats, steel rails, and hardwood posts. Snipers harassed us the whole while, forcing us to stop work and take cover from time to time.

I remember thinking that it was a good thing the Japs didn't have Seabees or our job would have been much tougher. As it was, the wooden pilings were easy for us to defeat. We didn't encounter anything as tough as what the Seabees had built for us train on in Fort Pierce.

The current was pretty strong and, when the tide went out, many of the landing ships and landing craft were left high and dry on the beaches. That slowed us down until the tide let us get out of there.

When we got to Borneo, there wasn't much for us to do but get bad sunburns and sit waiting.

Dirty water lapped at the beaches, which were littered with war wreckage. Here you can see a pontoon bridge.

Tides and strong currents often left LCIs high and dry on the beaches. Here you can see a few of the obstacles left.

The water was was brown with polution and stank, but we still had to take out those obstacles.

165

Name **DAWSON, willaim Louis**
(Name in Full, Surname to the Left)

256,52 66   Rate **GM2c**
(Service No.)

Date Reported Aboard: **28 August 1944**

USS LCI (D) 228 NCDU"2
(Present Ship or Station)

RB NVay 167
(Ship or Station Received From)

**Authorized to wear Asiatic-Pacific
area service ribbon with 6ne star
Auth:Cominch USFleet ltr,FF1/P15
serial 13,1-2-1945**

**Authorized to wear Philippine
Liberation ribbon with two stars.
Auth:AlNav, 64 Of 1945**

R. M. Kearns
R. M. Kearns
Lt. (jg) USNR
Commanding

 # 11

**Participated in operations four d
prior to and initial landings on
Tarakan I., Borneo, NEI, from
April 27 to May 1, 1945.**

R. M. Kearns
R. M. Kearns
Lt. (jg) USNR
Commanding

Date Transferred_____

To_____

_____
Signature and Rank of Officer Authorized to Sign

Date Received Aboard:_____

_____
(New Ship or Station)

_____
(Last Ship or Station)

_____
Signature and Rank of Officer Authorized to Sign

ORIGINAL
FOR SERVICE RECORD

Borneo was rich in oil, and the Japanese sure exploited it. They didn't care what mess they made. The water coming out of the rivers was dirty and contaminated by the industrial activity. We were stuck at that stinking end of the world with nothing to do. We pulled some LSTs off sandbars and kept up with our training. We had two men fall overboard, and I jumped in and saved them. Compared to what we had been through, saving a couple of lives wasn't that exciting. After liberating most of the islands in the Pacific, we were all waiting for and dreading the big event: Invading Japan itself.

Our final mission was doing some light reconnaissance work in Brunei Bay. We were done by June 10, 1945.

On June 11, the orders we were waiting for came through. We were to return to the United States for cold-water training so that we could be ready for the invasion of Japan in the fall.

We boarded the *USS Kline* (APD-120) for transit to Morotai, where we transferred to LCI 228 for transit to Leyte. After changing to yet another LCI, we were taken to the Naval Receiving Station on Samar, which is a large island on the eastern reaches of the Philippines. Our orders were to then embark on the *USS Magoffin* (APA-199), for transit to Honolulu.

While we were getting ready to leave Samar, Johnny Wilhide came down with a bad case of malaria. In all the time we were together, none of us had gotten seriously injured or sick. Now, with a ship ready to take us home, here was Johnny, as sick as I have ever seen anyone. We had trained together and spent two years together in some pretty tough situations. We just looked at each other and knew there was no way we were going home without him.

Our orders were to be aboard ship at 7:00 the morning of June 3. We decided to make one last-minute goodbye visit to Johnny in the hospital that morning. When we walked out, we intended to walk out with him. We brought clothes for Johnny and were ready to prop him up, but he was in pretty bad shape. I don't know if he cared to live or die at that moment, and was as limp as a ragdoll. We gave up on dressing him and walking him out. Instead, we wrapped him up in a sheet and one of us heaved him over his shoulder like a sack of dirty laundry. We acted like we knew what we were doing and no one stopped us to ask questions. We boarded the ship without anyone taking much

WILLIAMS-DAWSON PRINDOPONY

Between operations in Borneo.

DAWSON

Relaxing by a gun tub.

WILHIDE   DAWSON

I am not sure where we are, but here we are enjoying some well-earned cold beers somewhere civilized.

Bill Dawson GM2c 1945

notice. We couldn't take Johnny to our berths because he was so sick. Instead, we slipped into sick bay and found a nice clean bed for him. We kept watch, hoping no one would notice him until it was too late. The minutes passed as slowly as you could possibly imagine.

When the ship began to vibrate, we took heart. It was then that the ship's doctor came in. We explained what we had done—slowly, mind you. We needed every minute. That doctor didn't waste any time in going straight to the commanding officer of the ship. By then, all the lines had already been dropped we were away from the pier and getting under way.

We got an extra-special chewing out, but that didn't bother us. It was the duty of the CO to be angry, and we were ready to take our punishment. It was worth it, especially since our plan had worked. There was no going back to the dock. Johnny was coming home with us.

Within five days, Johnny was as good as new. We waited for our punishment, but it never came. We never heard another thing about it, and the incident never appeared in any of our records.

The trip home was uneventful. All of us looked forward to seeing our families again. We had orders to report back to Fort Pierce, and then we knew we would soon return to the West Coast to start cold-water training. Beyond that, we knew Japan waited. We didn't look forward to it.

We arrived in Honolulu on July 15, and boarded an Amphibious Attack Transport or APA bound for San Francisco.

Getting back to the East Coast wasn't so easy. With all the invasion preparations under way, everything was terribly overcrowded. We couldn't get on a train or airplane, and worried that we would spend our whole leave sitting in San Francisco.

LT Kaine saved the day. He started chatting with a lady who was in charge of doling out seats on the flights going east. He told her his name, rank, and organization. It turned out she had a brother in demolition. When she heard we were NCDU, she asked if we knew him. Actually—and fortunately—we did. He was in the Philippines with us and we had enjoyed a beer with him after an operation.

She said, "Oh, you poor boys," and immediately placed all twelve of us on an east-bound airplane. It was really great, because we got home fast and had a whole thirty days' leave. To be so close to home and then not to be able to get there would have been hard to take.

The Navy top brass didn't tell us much—just to get ready for Japan. I always did what I was told, even though a lot of it wasn't always good things or nice things. I didn't look forward to much of it. Now, facing the invasion of Japan was no different. It was something that had to be done.

I was in the Navy for what was called a "minority cruise." You go in at 17 and can get out at 21. By the time I got home, my service felt finished. I had had enough and had seen all I wanted to see. The idea of going back

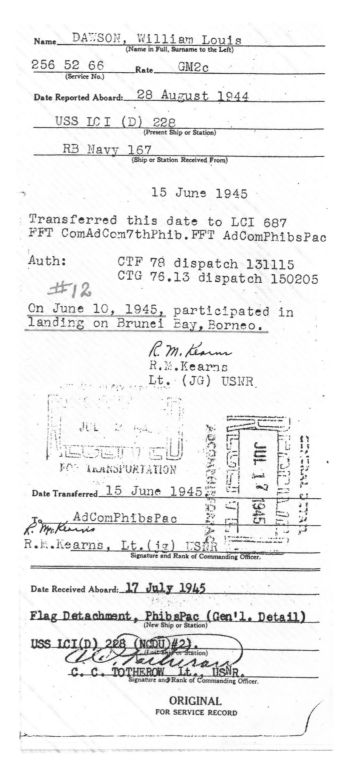

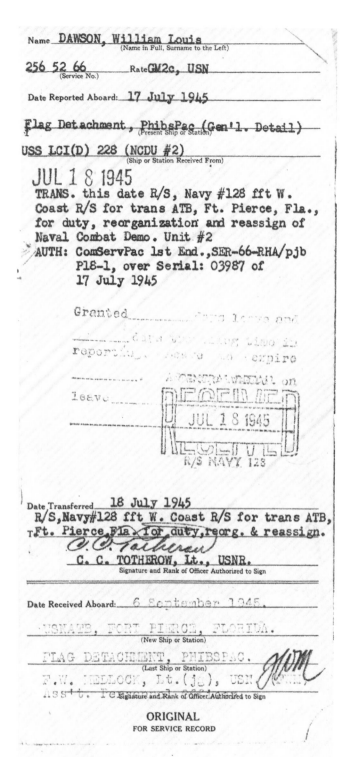

seemed unreal. I just wanted what we had done to be done, and I didn't want the outfit I was in to carry on without me. It was just us and always only just us. I couldn't see others taking our places. My heart wasn't in it, but I tried to get myself ready to return to the Pacific anyway.

We had heard rumors of a special bomb, but we didn't have any idea what this super weapon was about. The dropping of the A-bomb came as a surprise. I was in Washington, DC with my family, when I heard about bombing Hiroshima and Nagasaki. On Victory over Japan Day in August 1945, we got caught up in the jubilation like everyone else. For me personally, it was a very real relief.

Nonetheless, I had orders to go back to Fort Pierce. Pretty soon, I was on a train heading to Florida, but felt no dread. We were not going to train for the cold water! Instead, my time in Florida was a chance to see everyone again and say our proper good-byes. It felt right to take our leave where we had gotten our start down with the mosquitos and sand fleas. We wound things down and I was discharged. The war, my service, and the NCDUs were over.

Place of discharge .... PRNC, NGF, Washington, D. C.

Authority for discharge .... BuPers Manual, Article H-6206 (EE)

Serial or file number 256 52 66

Date and place of birth 18 April 1925 .... Washington, D. C.
                  (Date)   (Place)

Date of entry into active service ... Performed no active duty during this enlistment

Rating at discharge ... GMM2, V6 USNR

Total service for pay purposes during this enlistment 05 years, 00 months, 00 days

Service (vessels and stations served on) Performed no active duty during this enlistment

Remarks .... Enlisted: 15 May

Pers-E374-EKN-hc   THIS CERTIFICATE ADMINISTRATIVELY ISSUED BY THE BUREAU OF NAVAL
20 Oct 1952   PERSONNEL. THE DATA ON THIS DISCHARGE IS TAKEN FROM DAWSON'S
                    RECORD IN THE BUREAU.

                                                  J. R. MC MANUS, Lieutenant .... , U.S.N. (𝔇 ,
                                     By direction of Chief of Naval Personnel

I am always a bit taken aback when I read my official discharge papers. Our work was so secret that my record of service states: "Performed no active duty during this enlistment." I cannot for the life of me imagine any duty MORE active than the training we completed and work we did in the NCDUs.

Authority for discharge............ AlNAV 395-45

FOLLOWING DATA TRANSCRIBED FROM NAVPERS-553, NOTICE OF SEPARATION.

Serial or file number...... 256 52 66

Date and place of birth...... 4-18-25   Washington, D.C.
................................(Date)..................................(Place)

Date of entry into active service...... 4-14-43

Highest rank or rating held...... GM2c

Service (vessels and stations served on)...... USNTS, BAINBRIDGE, MD.; ATB, FORT PIERCE, FLA.; NAVAL
COMBAT DEMOLITION UNIT NO. 2; USS LCI(L)-228, NCDU #2; FLAG DETACHMENT, PHILSPA
USNATB, FORT PIERCE, FLA.

Remarks...... MEDAL: Asiatic-Pacific Area & 5 star
Philippine Liberation & 2 stars
American Area
Victory-World War II

BIRTH CERTIFICATE NO. 283-971

.... K.R. WRIGHT, Ensign.........., U.S.

Other entries previously made hereon now covered by NavPers 553, Notice of Separation.

Eventually, some active duty service was added to my records.

NOTICE OF SEPARATION FROM U. S. NAVAL SERVICE

NAVPERS-553 (REV. 8-45)

1. SERIAL OR FILE NO.	2. NAME (LAST) (FIRST) (MIDDLE)	3. RATE AND CLASS/OR	5 PLACE OF SEPARATION
RANK AND CLASSIFICATION	4. PERMANENT ADDRESS FOR MAILING PURPOSES		USN PSC SHELTON, VIRGINIA

256 52 66 DAWSON, William Louis
GM2c USN
106 Summer Drive, Alexandria,
Independent City,   Va.

6. CHARACTER OF SEPARATION

Honorable

7. ADDRESS FROM WHICH EMPLOYMENT WILL BE SOUGHT

106 Summer Drive
Alexandria, Va.

8. RACE	9. SEX	10. MARITAL STATUS	11. U.S. CITIZEN (YES OR NO)	12. DATE AND PLACE OF BIRTH
White	M	Single	Yes	4-18-25 Washington, D.C.

	13. REGISTERED	14. SELECTIVE SERVICE BOARD OF REGISTRATION	15. HOME ADDRESS AT TIME OF ENTRY INTO SERVICE
Sel. Ser. Date	☐ YES ☒ NO		1801 "B" St., S.E. Wash., D.C.

16. MEANS OF ENTRY (INDICATE BY CHECK IN APPROPRIATE BOX)	17. DATE OF ENTRY INTO ACTIVE SERVICE	18. NET SERVICE (FOR PAY PURPOSES) (YRS., MOS., DAYS)
☒ ENLISTED ☐ INDUCTED ☐ COMMISSIONED	4-14-43	2 11 24
DATE 4-14-43 DATE DATE		

19. PLACE OF ENTRY INTO ACTIVE SERVICE

Washington, D.C.

20. QUALIFICATIONS, CERTIFICATES HELD, ETC.	21. RATINGS HELD	22. FOREIGN AND/OR SEA SERVICE WORLD WAR II
See Rating Description Booklet For GM2c	AS, S2c, GM3c, GM2c	☒ YES ☐ NO

24. SERVICE (VESSELS AND STATIONS SERVED ON)

23. SERVICE SCHOOLS COMPLETED	WEEKS
ATB, FORT PIERCE, FLA (DEMOLITION)	8

USNTS, BAINBRIDGE, MD.; ATB, FORT
PIERCE, FLA.; NAVAL COMBAT DEMOLITION
UNIT NO. 2; USS LCI(L)-228, NCDU #2;
FLAG DETACHMENT, PHIBSPAC; USNATB, FORT
PIERCE, FLA.

IMPORTANT: IF PREMIUM IS NOT PAID WHEN DUE OR WITHIN THIRTY-ONE DAYS THEREAFTER, INSURANCE WILL LAPSE. MAKE CHECKS OR MONEY ORDERS PAYABLE TO THE TREASURER OF THE U. S. AND FORWARD TO COLLECTOR'S SUBDIVISION, VETERAN'S ADMINISTRATION, WASHINGTON 25, D. C.

25. KIND OF INSURANCE	26. EFFECTIVE MONTH OF ALLOTMENT DISCONTINUANCE	27. MO. NEXT PREMIUM DUE	28. AMOUNT OF PREMIUM DUE EACH MONTH	29. INTENTION OF VETERAN TO CONTINUE INS.
N	Apr 46	May 46	6.40	Yes

30. TOTAL PAYMENT UPON DISCHARGE	31. TRAVEL OR MILEAGE ALLOWANCE INCLUDED IN TOTAL PAYMENT	32. INITIAL MUSTERING OUT	33. NAME OF DISBURSING OFFICER
$ 124.37	$ 10.50	100.00	P.A. TREMBLAY LT (JG)SC USN

34. REMARKS

"Point System"
MEDALS: Asiatic-Pacific Area & 5 stars;
     Philippine Liberation & 2
     stars; American Area; Victory-
     World War II
     Good Conduct (affidivat)

35. SIGNATURE (BY DIRECTION OF COMMANDING OFFICER)

L. J. SNYDER, Lt.Comdr., USNR.

36. NAME AND ADDRESS OF LAST EMPLOYER	37. DATES OF LAST EMPL'MT.	38. MAIN CIVILIAN OCCUPATION AND D. O. T. NO.
Washington Naval Yard Washington, D. C.	FROM 6-42 TO 4-43	Patternmaker, Wood 5-17 . 020

39. JOB PREFERENCE (LIST TYPE, LOCALITY, AND GENERAL AREA)	40. PREFERENCE FOR ADDITIONAL TRAINING (TYPE OF TRAINING)
Student Washington, D. C.	Motion Picture Operating

44. VOCATIONAL OR TRADE COURSES (NATURE AND LENGTH OF COURSE)

Mill Shop-3 Yrs.
Cabinet Making-3 Yrs.

41. NON-SERVICE EDU. (YRS. SUCCESSFULLY COMPLETED)	42. DEGREES	43. MAJOR COURSE OR FIELD
GRAM.: 8 H.S.: 4 COLL.: 0	None	General

45. RIGHT INDEX FINGERPRINT	46. OFF DUTY EDUCATIONAL COURSES COMPLETED

4/17/46	William L Dawson
47. DATE OF SEPARATION	**48. SIGNATURE OF PERSON BEING SEPARATED**

173

Honorable Discharge

from the
United States Navy

This is to certify that

WILLIAM LOUIS DAWSON _____ a GUNNER'S MATE SECOND CLASS _____

is **Honorably Discharged** *from the* U.S. NAVAL PERSONNEL SEPARATION CENTER _____

SHELTON, VIRGINIA _____ *and from the Naval Service of the United States*

this 17th *day of* April 1946 _____

This certificate is awarded as a Testimonial of Fidelity and Obedience.

_____

K.K. WRIGHT, Ensign, USNR,
Administrative Assistant,
By direction of the Commanding Officer.

RS. 660 (REVISED AUGUST 1945)

Chapter 9
Honoring and Remembering

Serving my country has been my great privilege and honor. To know that the brave men I trained and fought with in Class 1 had laid the foundation for the future Navy SEALs and other great warriors in the Naval Special Warfare community is a distinction that I bear with great humility. I am in awe of how each generation has carried forward what we started and has added their own marks.

I enjoyed staying in touch with the men of Class 1, and the men who have followed us in this tradition. I especially enjoy shaking the hands and looking in the eyes of the newest SEALs. That my country still produces such men is a matter of great pride to me.

During the time of my service, I didn't think much past the next operation, and never imagined having a place in history. I kept my scrapbook for my own remembrance and to share a piece of who I am with friends and special people I have met. Publishing it now allows me to document and share the stories of the Pacific NCDUs more widely.

THE UDT—SEAL MUSEUM

Dedicated
November 10, 1985

Preserving the Past to Ensure the Future

UDT-SEAL MUSEUM, P.O. BOX 1117, FT. PIERCE, FL 33454   407-464-FROG

When I got the call from CAPT Norman Olson telling me of the founding of a Museum
for our community, I jumped right in. I am a founder and life member.

Over the years, I have been a frequent visitor and have contributed a number of artifacts I saved during my service during World War II.

177

UDT/SEAL MUSEUM ASSOCIATION
BOARD OF DIRECTORS

Capt. L.W. Bailey USN, (Ret), President
E.F. Andy Andrews, Vice President
H. Aschenbrenner, Secretary/Treasurer

Rolly Pastermack   George Nash
J.D. Watson, QMCS, USN, (Ret)   Bud Grant
Al Stankie   Cdr. J. Dilley USN

UDT/SEAL MUSEUM STAFF
Jim Adams, Curator   Jim Watson, Assistant Curator
Robert Edgel

VOLUNTEERS

Lloyd Biddle	Peter Hartmen
Ken Mattews	Don Minchew
Claude Clefton	Bill Martino
Jacquelyn Campbell	Mary Vorees

Unholy Four Association
Donald Feindt, Ex. Dir.
Dedication of Guadalcanal Beach Head

PANAMA MEMORIAL

Dedicated in memory of	Families' Escort from Seal Team 4
LTjg John Patrick Connors	LTjg Hall
ENC Donald L. McFaul	HMC Knauff
BMI Christopher Taylor Tilghman	RM_2 Plank
TM_2 Isaac George Rodriguez	GMGS Hansen

Music by Navy Gleeclub Orlando NRTC

Parachute Jump by Navy Leap Frogs Jump Team
All Jumpers are Navy SEALS

Drill Team Exhibition
NTC Orlando Drill Team

Simulated Dog Fight
Vintage Aircraft Association

Supporting Units
Boy Scouts of America
Seacadets

CEREMONY

Presentation of the Colors
Orlando NTC Color Guard

National Anthem
Glee Club

Invocation
Monsignor Irvine Nugent

Welcome and Acknowledge Special Guest
President UDT/SEAL Museum Association
Capt. Larry Bailey USN, (Ret)

Dedication and Unveiling of Team Plaques
NCDU 2 & 3 William Dawson   UDT 11 Robert Wells
UDT 7 Sid Robbins   UDT 18 Joe Anlauf

Bell Ceremony for Members
Who Have Passed on in the Last Year

Navy Hymn
Glee Club

Presentation of World War II
Philippines Surrender Document and Sword
Mrs. Elizabeth Bush & Dr. Draper Kauffman, Jr.

Remarks & Unveiling of Panama Memorial
Commodore Naval Special Warfare Group 2
Commodore L. Boink

Rifle Volleys
SEAL Team 4 Honor Guard

Taps
Dedicating Prayer by Coast Guard Chaplin
LT Thomas Klappert

God Bless America
Glee Club

Memorial Designed and Built by "Ozzie" Grant

In 1990, the members of NCDU -2 and NCDU-3 funded a bronze plaque with our names, major unclassified missions, and dates of service, which was dedicated at the annual Veteran's Day Muster.

NoV 1991

UNITED STATES NAVY
CLASS #1
NAVAL COMBAT DEMOLITION UNITS

JULY 2, 1943 TO OCTOBER 9, 1945
FORT PIERCE, FL

NCDU #2

KAINE, FRANK R.	LT.	BRATTLEBORO VERMONT
ARMSTRONG, WILLIAM J.	C.M.	BEAVERTON OREGON
PIERCE, ALAR H.	MM 1/C	ANNISTON ALABAMA
DAWSON, WILLIAM L.	GM 2/C	WASHINGTON D.C.
WILLIAMS, DILLIARD J.	GM 2/C	NORTH CAROLINA
WILHIDE, JONNY N.	GM 2/C	NORTH CAROLINA

NCDU #3

ANDERSON, LLOYD E.	LT.	LOS ANGELES CALIFORNIA
DE VRIES, CORNELIUS C.	ACOM	SEATTLE WASHINGTON
SANDY, JAMES O.	GM 2/C	WASHINGTON D.C.
PAHDOPUNY, SAM	GM 2/C	LAWTON OKLAHOMA
MESSALL, EDWARD A.	GM 2/C	MARLOW OKLAHOMA
ESKRIDGE, HARRISON O.	GM 2/C	RUTHERFORDTON N.C.

NEW GUINEA	PHILIPPINES	BORNEO
ADMIRALTY ISLANDS	LEYTE	TARAKAN
AITAPE	MINDORO	BRUNEI BAY
BIAK	LINGAYEN GULF	
NOEMFOOR	ZAMBOANGA	
	TALISAY CEBU	
	MINDANAO	

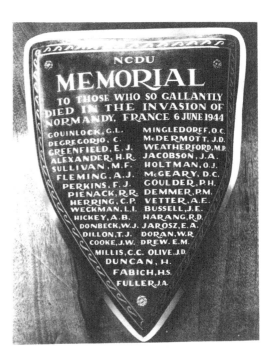

NCDU
MEMORIAL
TO THOSE WHO SO GALLANTLY
DIED IN THE INVASION OF
NORMANDY, FRANCE 6 JUNE 1944

GOUINLOCK, G.L.	MINGLEDORFF, O.C.
DEGREGORIO, C.	McDERMOTT, J.D.
GREENFIELD, E.J.	WEATHERFORD, M.P.
ALEXANDER, H.R.	JACOBSON, J.A.
SULLIVAN, M.F.	HOLTMAN, O.J.
FLEMING, A.J.	McGEARY, D.C.
PERKINS, F.J.	GOULDER, P.H.
PIENACK, R.R.	DEMMER, P.M.
HERRING, C.P.	VETTER, A.E.
WECKMAN, L.I.	BUSSELL, J.E.
HICKEY, A.B.	HARANG, R.D.
DONBECK, W.J.	JAROSZ, E.A.
DILLON, T.J.	DORAN, W.R.
COOKE, J.W.	DREW, E.M.
MILLIS, C.C.	OLIVE, J.D.
DUNCAN, H.	
FABICH, H.S.	
FULLER, J.A.	

Visitors to the National Navy UDT-SEAL Museum in Fort Pierce, Florida can see our plaque, our artifacts, and even some of the flags pictured in this book that we captured on our missions.

NOV 1991

Key for Pacific Operations

1	GREEN ISLANDS	NCDU 4, 5
2	EMIRAU ST. MATTIAS	NCDU 4, 5
3	ADMIRALTY ISLANDS	NCDU 2, 3
4	AITAPE NEW GUINEA	NCDU 2, 3
5	BIAK	NCDU 2, 3
6	NOEMFOOR	NCDU 2, 3
7	KWAJALEIN	UDT 1; NCDU 6, 7, 8; S & R
8	ROI-NAMUR	UDT 2; NCDU 6, 7, 8
9	ENIWETOK	UDT 1; NCDU 6, 7, 8
10	ULITHI	UDT 10
11	YAP	
12	PELELIU PALAU	UDT 6, 7, 8; NCDU 4, 5
13	ANGAUR PALAU	UDT 8, 10
14	SAIPAN	UDT 5, 7; S & R
15	TINIAN	UDT 5, 7
16	GUAM	UDT 3, 4, 6; S & R
17	LEYTE P.I.	UDT 3, 4, 5, 6, 8, 9, 10; NCDU 2, 3
18	MINDORO P.I.	NCDU 2, 3
19	LINGAYEN GULF	UDT 5, 8, 9, 10, 14, 15; NCDU 2, 3
20	MINDANAO P.I.	NCDU 2, 3
21	CEBU P.I.	NCDU 2, 3
22	POLLOCK, MINDANAO	NCDU 23
23	SUBIC BAY P.I.	UDT 10
24	IWO JIMA	UDT 12, 13, 14, 15; S & R
25	KERAMA RETTO	UDT 12, 13, 14, 19
26	OKINAWA	UDT 4, 7, 11, 12, 13, 14, 16, 17, 21; S & R
27	TARAKAN, BORNEO	NCDU 2, 3
28	BRUNEI BAY	UDT 11; NCDU 2, 3
29	BALIKPAPAN BORNEO	UDT 11, 18

S & R = SCOUTS & RAIDERS
UDT = UNDERWATER DEMOLITION TEAM
NCDU = NAVAL COMBAT DEMOLITION UNIT

NEW GUINEA 1944

I am pleased to see the National Navy UDT-SEAL Museum in Fort Pierce welcomes visitors with the statue called "The Naked Warrior." The statue depicts combat swimmers like us, standing on a "horned scully," a beach obstacle we trained to demolish. The statue was designed at the famous Johnson Atelier, which is J. Seward Johnson, Jr.'s workshop in Philadelphia. It was officially unveiled on November 12, 1988.

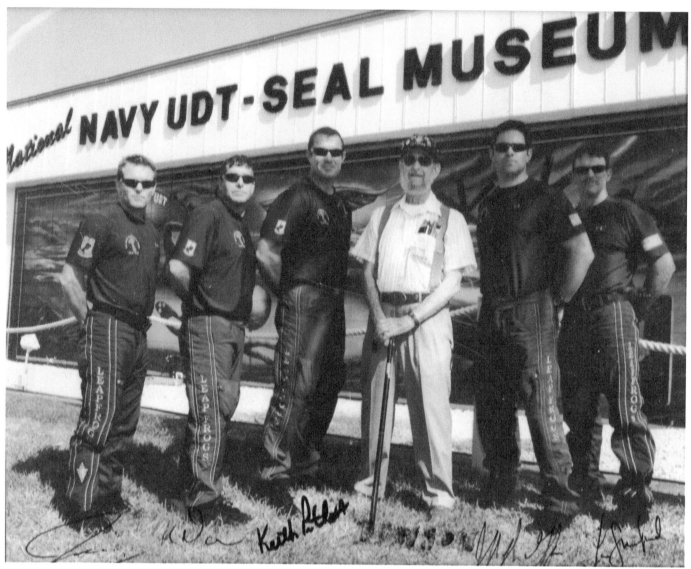

We didn't have air capabilities when I was on the teams, so it was fun to meet some of today's SEALs, who are members of the Leap Frogs U.S. Navy Parachute Team.

My brick is on the front walkway entrance to the Navy SEAL Museum.

I joined other legacy unit veterans to place a commemorative plaque at Arlington National Cemetery in 1992.

IN MEMORY OF OUR FALLEN COMRADES WHO SACRIFICED THEIR LIVES IN THE SERVICE OF THEIR COUNTRY WHILE SERVING IN THE UNITED STATES NAVY WITH NAVAL COMBAT DEMOLITION UNITS AND UNDERWATER DEMOLITION TEAMS, DURING WORLD WAR II

The President and the Board of Directors
UDT-SEAL Association
invite you to attend the
President's Reception
on Saturday, July 18, 1998 at 5:30 p.m.
Naval Amphibious Base, Snug Harbor Club

Dress: Casual

R.S.V.P: (757) 363-7490
or
udtseal.infi.net

William L. Dawson
9450 Silver Oak Road
La Plata, MD 20646

I have been honored to attend many World War II commemmoration ceremonies, including one in Fort Pierce; memorializing the now-closed base there.

The

General William Smallwood Chapter, TROA
Charlotte Hall Veterans Home
Charles County Commissioners
invite you and a guest to attend
a celebration
commemorating the
50th Anniversary of V-J Day

Sunday, August 13, 1995, 2:00 p.m.

Salute to USO - Port Tobacco Players
Award of Commendation Certificates
will be presented

—Guest Speaker—
General Andrew J. Goodpaster

Refreshments following program

―――――――――――――

Space is limited; please respond by July 31.
Charles County Department of Community Services
(301) 934-0107
Charlotte Hall Veterans Home
(301) 884-8171, ext. 402
Please provide name, number, and number attending.

The Vice President
requests the pleasure of
your company at the
National Commemoration
of the fiftieth anniversary
of V-J Day
on Saturday, September 2, 1995
at ten o'clock
at Summerall Field
Fort Myer, Virginia

Washington, D.C.
Commemoration
of the fiftieth anniversary
of V-J Day,
on Saturday,
September 2, 1995.
Please present this ticket
with identification
upon arrival at the
ceremony site.

NOT TRANSFERRABLE

The Commander, Office of Naval Intelligence
requests the pleasure of your company at a Retirement Ceremony
in honor of
Captain Peter I. "BULL FROG" Wikul, USN
on Friday, the twenty-fifth of September two thousand and nine
at ten o'clock
hosted by Naval Special Warfare Group FOUR
Little Creek Naval Amphibious Base
Norfolk, Virginia

This ceremony will include the turnover of the BULL FROG from the
"Last Man Standing," East Coast UDT/SEAL Training, Class UDTR 7102
to Admiral Eric T. Olson.

R.S.V.P. by 18 September 2009
301-669-3007 or dmcnamara@nmic.navy.mil

Military guests: Summer White
Civilian guests: Business

I am standing next to the "Bull Frog," a trophy given to the NSW operator who has served the longest. Navy CAPT Pete Wikul passed the title of "Bull Frog" to Navy ADM Eric T. Olson, who was commander of U.S. Special Operations Command at the time. The Bull Frog title is awarded regardless of rank.

I was delighted to congratulate CAPT Peter Wikul on his retirement. I enjoy every opportunity to represent the legacy component in our community.

I enjoyed meeting CAPT Chuck Wolf.

I am an admirer of ADM Eric Olson. I get a kick seeing so many Navy SEAL flag officers. When I was in the service, our top-ranking officer was a junior lieutenant.

Rudy Bosch is a friend I always enjoy seeing.

Me with RADM Tom Richards (Retired).

Statue RAFFLE Results

RAFFLE
"RUN AND A SWIM STATUE"

Proceeds from Raffle for the construction of the UDT/Seal Memorial Park to be built at the Naval Amphibious Base, Little Creek, Virginia

Phone: (804) 481-1276

Donation: $20.00

Raffle will be held upon sale of 400 tickets. Winner will be contacted by phone and announced in "Blast".

900

The raffle of the "Run and Swim" bronze statue was held during this year's F.O. UDT/SEAL Reunion at Little Creek, VA. The winning ticket was No. 24 (new issued ticket) was held by **William Dawson** of LaPlate, MD. When we announced the winning ticket number, I never saw a happier person. You could have sworn that he had won the state lottery.

I want to thank all who contributed to the raffle. We were able to raise just under $5,000 for the UDT/SEAL Memorial Park.

Joe Dearing

Memorabilia Addition!

Dear Sir:

On July 17, 1994, I was the lucky winner of the Bronze Statue "Run and Swim" that was raffled at the Fraternal Order UDT/SEAL reunion picnic. I feel honored to have this wonderful statue.

I was in the first class to train for underwater demolition at Fort Pierce, Florida in July and August of 1943. My Commanding Officer was Draper L. Kaufman. After our training NCDU 2 & 3 were shipped to the Pacific where we participated in twelve (12) operations.

Attached is a brief history of these operations.

Sincerely,

William L. Dawson
9450 Silver Oak Road
La Plata, MD 20646

Editor's Note: *William Dawson is not new to the **BLAST**. We were fortunate enough to run Shane Artim's feature of him in our March 1993 issue (Volume 25, Number 1). What a great item to add to his wall of memorabilia.*

Brief History of NCDU # 2 & 3 World War II
Participated in the following operations in the Southwest Pacific.

#1   March 9th to 23rd 1944
     Admiralty Islands, Bismarck Archipelreo

#2   April 19th to 24th 1944
     Aitape, New Guinea

#3   May 25th to June 6, 1944
     Biak Island, New Guinea

#4   June 30 to July 8, 1944
     Noomfoor Island, New Guinea
     Received commendation

#5   October 20, 1944 initial landing
     Leyte Island, Philippines

#6   December 15, 1944
     Mindoro Philippines

U.S. NAVY U.D.T. COMBAT TEAM II   *William L. Dawson, WWII*

Of all the commemorations and memorials around the world, I enjoyed my own place of rememembrance in my home office the most. Here I could think of dear friends and dangerous days quietly.

My decorations include the Combat Action Ribbon, WWII Victory Medal, Asian-Pacific Campaign Medal, WWII American Campaign Medal, and the Navy Good Conduct Medal.

The ribbon rows above the UDT patch: Top row: WWII American Campaign Ribbon; Asian Pacific Campaign Ribbon (with four bronze stars – indicating four separate campaigns). Bottom row: WWII Victory Ribbon and the Good Conduct Ribbon.

World War II Commemorative

CERTIFICATE OF APPRECIATION

is Awarded to

William L. Dawson

this 13th of February, 1994
for outstanding service to The United States of America
during the years 1941 through 1945
on the 50th Anniversary of World War II

BE IT KNOWN TO ALL HERE PRESENT
THAT UPON THIS 27th DAY OF June 2003, THIS
2002 DEFENDER OF THE CONSTITUTION AWARD
IS GIVEN TO

William L. Dawson

IN RECOGNITION OF MERITORIOUS SERVICE TO OUR NATION AND THE PRINCIPLES
EMBODIED IN OUR BILL OF RIGHTS, ABOVE AND BEYOND THE CALL OF DUTY.
BY UNANIMOUS DECLARATION OF THE
DEFENDER OF THE CONSTITUTION AWARD EXECUTIVE COMMITTEE:

WAYNE, R. LAPIERRE, JR.

World War II Commemorative

Certificate of Appreciation

is Awarded to

William L. Dawson

"A Grateful Nation Remembers"
your sacrifices and service during
World War II.

_____
Charles County Board of Commissioners
Murray D. Levy, President

_____
The Gen. Wm. Smallwood Chapter, TROA
President Robert M. Pender, Capt. USN, Ret.

City of Bowie

CERTIFICATE OF APPRECIATION

is Awarded to

WILLIAM DAWSON

**for outstanding support to the
Department of Defense Commemoration for
the 50th Anniversary of World War II**

_____
Mayor

_____
Chairperson

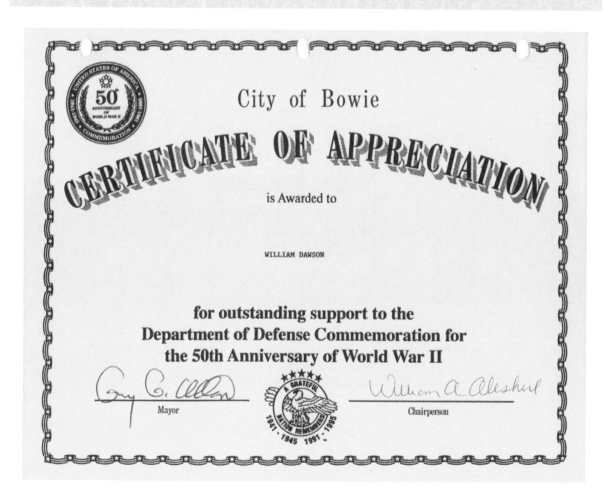

August 13, 1993

Dear Bill,

It was great to meet you at the UDT SEAL reunion and the fiftieth anniversary of the Navy Combat Demolition Units and Underwater Demolition Teams. Your scrapbook is truly a remarkable historical reference. I was very impressed with it. The Japanese leaflets you had were very interesting.

I've given your name to our Director of Psychological Operations and Civil Affairs. I've told him about your leaflets. I suspect either someone from our PSYOPS Directorate, or someone from our 4th Psychological Operations Group in Fort Bragg, North Carolina, may contact you. They will probably ask to see and perhaps make copies of your Japanese leaflets. If they do, I am the source of their interest, and I just wanted to give you a heads-up.

Again, Bill, it was good to meet you in Little Creek, and I look forward to seeing you again in November at Fort Pierce.

Sincerely,
and fire in the hole

Irve C. Le Moyne
Rear Admiral, U.S. Navy

Mr. William L. Dawson
Box 4082 Silver Oak Road
La Plata, Maryland 20645

August 7, 1995

Dear Bill,

Thank you very much for your kind and thoughtful words and your card. And also, thank you for the frogman magnet.

I have heard lots of good reports about this year's UDT/SEAL Reunion and the demonstration. I'm glad it all went so well.

Things are going very well for me, and I expect to be at the Reunion at Fort Pierce this Fall. So, I will look forward to seeing you there. Meanwhile, Bill, take care.

Sincerely,

Irve C. Le Moyne
Rear Admiral, U.S. Navy

March 14, 1995

Dear Bill,

First off, let me apologize for not responding to your letter of September 9, 1993. Somehow the entire package you sent got filed away, and it just resurfaced.

I was surprised and very pleased to receive the Japanese leaflets included with your letter. They are true pieces of history, and I will treasure them.

You requested a copy of a letter I read at the UDT/SEAL Reunion in Little Creek. Unfortunately, I have not been able to locate that letter, and I cannot recall what it said. Can you refresh my memory?

Bill, again, my apologies for not getting back to you sooner.

Sincerely,

Irve C. Le Moyne
Rear Admiral, U.S. Navy

Mr. William L. Dawson
Rt. 4, Box 4082
Silver Oak Road
LaPlata, MD 20646

RECEIPT FOR LOANS   4-24 , 1987

Received from WILLIAM L. DAWSON   Tel ( )

Address RT-4   BOX 4082   LA PLATA   MD.   20646
                (Street)   (City)   (State)   (Zip)

The following item(s) for a period from 4-24-87 To 4-24-92

Accession No.	Description
87.23.1	(16) ASSORTED PHOTOS
87.23.2	(5) COMICS

It is my understanding that the above items loaned to the UDT-SEAL Museum Association, Inc., are subject to the conditions described on the reverse side.	Received for the UDT-SEAL Museum Assoc., Inc.
	By R. COOK (PRES.)
	Date
	Received for the UDT-SEAL Museum
By	By James F. Adams
Date	Date 4-24-87

E SIGNED UPON RETURN OF ITEMS

Received from the UDT-SEAL Museum Association, Inc. the above listed Items.

By _____   Date _____

DEFENSE AND ARMED FORCES AFFAIRS OFFICE
EMBASSY OF THE PHILIPPINES
1600 Massachusetts Ave., N.W.
Washington, D.C. 20036

November 20, 1994

Mr. William L. Dawson
9450 Silver Oak Road
La Plata, MD 20646

Dear Mr. Dawson,

We are pleased to send the Philippine Liberation Medal (PLM), and Philippine Republic Presidential Unit Citation Badge (PRPUCB) awarded to you by the Armed Forces of the Philippines. Please find the enclosed medal, and badge.

The Government of the Republic of the Philippines and the Filipino people greatly appreciate your role in helping us preserve the peace and freedom we now enjoy, and hope that you will continue to support our efforts in containing the problems that currently beset us.

Thank you very much for this chance to be of service to you and we wish you continued good health and prosperity.

Very truly yours,

JOSE M CALIMLIM
Colonel, PA (GSC)
Military Attache/Veterans Affairs Officer

Incl:

As stated

DEFENSE AND ARMED FORCES AFFAIRS OFFICE
Embassy of the Philippines
1617 Massachusetts Avenue, NW
Washington, D.C. 20036

30 October 1990

Mr. William L. Dawson
Rt. 4 Box 4082 Silver Oak Rd
La Plata, MD 20646

Dear Mr. Dawson:

This in connection with your request for the award of the Philippine Liberation Medal. Please find the enclosed medal. We hope it will serve your purpose.

We regret the unfortunate delay, the Government of the Republic Philippines and the Filipino people greatly appreciate your role in helping us preserve the peace and freedom we now enjoy. We hope that you will continue to support our efforts in containing the problems that currently beset us.

Should you have future query, please contact Mr. Ben Palomo at (202) 462-1770.

We thank you for your patience, cooperation and understanding.

Very truly yours,

FOR THE DEFENSE ATTACHE:

WARLINO J SADIARIN
Captain, PN (GSC)
Naval Attache/Vets Affairs Officer

Inclosure:

As stated

Obituaries

Captain Francis Riley Kaine

Captain Francis Riley Kaine, U. S. Naval Reserve, Retired, died of cancer at his home in Coronado, July 7 1999.

Capt. Kaine was a pioneer of Naval Special Warfare. He built men as well as underwater demolition charges. He served in the Navy for 28 years, with assignments in the Pacific, Atlantic, Caribbean, and Mediterranean.

Capt. Kaine was born February 13, 1920 in Brattleboro, VT. He was a graduate of Loyola College in Montreal, Canada and was studying for an advanced degree at the University of Rochester when World War II interrupted his academics.

During his subsequent naval career, Capt. Kaine saw what is now known as Naval Special Warfare (NSW) through many changes —

adaptations he frequently helped conceive and often helped put into place. A true founder of the NSW community, he was a plank owner of the World War II Naval Combat Demolition Units (NCDU), and a participant in the first NSW training Hell Week. He later played key leadership roles in nursing the fledgling NSW force through the dangers of peacetime budget cuts and helping it rise above the stresses of wartime growing pains.

Capt. Kaine's Navy career spanned some of the most intense wartime activities in NSW history. As an ensign, he was a founding member of the WW II NCDUs. He graduated in the first NCDU training class at Ft. Pierce, Fla. and deployed to the Southwest Pacific as officer-in-charge of NCDU-2, where they were the first NCDU training graduates to see combat in any WWII theater. There, known as "MacArthur's Frogman," he also acted as the senior NCDU officer in General MacArthur's Seventh Fleet Amphibious Forces, coordinating the operations of five other NCDUs. He participated directly in 12 amphibious landings and coordinated NCDU participation in 24 others.

After the war, Capt. Kaine returned to civilian life. He was recalled to active duty in late 1950 as a lieutenant commander when conflict flared in Korea and soon took command of Underwater Demolition Team TWO (UDT-2) at the Naval Amphibious Base, Little Creek, Virg. He subsequently commanded UDT-21, and Underwater Demolition Unit TWO. He played a key role in sustaining and advancing NSW during a time when its continued existence was a constant struggle. Some of the

innovations during this time were the introduction of submersibles to UDT and the use of helicopter and parachute techniques for swimmer delivery.

From 1958 to 1962, Capt. Kaine became chief of staff for personnel to commander Caribbean Sea Frontier/commandant TENTH Naval District/Commander Antilles Defense Command in Puerto Rico. In 1962 he returned to Little Creek to command Beachmaster Unit Two. From 1964 to 1966 he was the director, Special Operations Department at the Naval Amphibious School, Little Creek, which included UDT training, counterinsurgency training, and SERE (Survival, Evasion, Resistance, and Escape) training.

From December 9, 1966 to May 1, 1970, when he retired, Capt. Kaine was Commander, Naval Operations Support Group Pacific (during his tenure this became Naval Special Warfare Group Pacific) at the Naval Amphibious Base in Coronado. Here he oversaw personnel requirements and development of techniques, equipment, and weapons to counter enemy capabilities in the Vietnam conflict. While Vietnam was his primary focus, he also made planning and coordination trips to Thailand, Taiwan and Korea. During this final assignment he worked with industry, the intelligence community, Special Forces, Air Commandos, the Central Intelligence Agency, and Korean, Australian and various other foreign personnel. His primary responsibilities were to train, equip, manage, finance and transport three UDTs, one SEAL Team, one Beach Jumper Unit, a Boat Support Unit, and a Naval Special Warfare Group staff in the conduct of NSW operations in

Vietnam. Under his leadership, the size of the organization more than doubled during this time and the commitment to Southeast Asia increased by 1,500 percent.

The headquarters of commander, Naval Special Warfare Command in Coronado CA was named in his honor in March 1991.

During his service, Capt. Kaine was awarded the Legion of Merit, the Bronze Star medal with combat "V," the Presidential Unit Citation, and the Navy Unit Citation, as well as a variety of campaign and service ribbons.

After he retired from the Navy, Capt. Kaine initially worked as a military consultant for Atlantic Research Corporation and then for Ocean Marketing Consulting Corporation. From 1975 through 1979, he was executive director of the Chamber of Commerce in Coronado. From 1980 to 1986 he was a manager for the Bank of Coronado. He retired for good in June 1986. Capt. Kaine was active in Rotary until he retired.

Capt. Kaine is survived by his wife of 56 years, the former Jeanne Audrey Dyer, and five children (Michael, [Candace Bridget, their second child preceded him in death], Carey (Durham), Candace (Boniwell), and Claudia (Natter), and Carole (Kraft)) and 13 grandchildren.

A memorial mass will be held at the North Island Naval Air Station Chapel today, Wednesday, July 14 at 1 pm. This will be followed by interment services at Ft Rosecrans National Cemetary at Pt Loma at 3 pm.

In lieu of flowers, the family requests that donations should be sent in Capt. Kaine's name to the UDT-SEAL Association, P.O. Box 5365, Virginia Beach, VA 234571.

James Daniel Sandy Sr.

JAMES DANIEL

SANDY SR., (JD)

James Daniel Sandy Sr., (JD), 88, of Wilmington passed away May 7, 2011, at New Hanover Regional Medical Center.

He was preceded in death by his wife, Dorothy E. Sandy.

JD is survived by his son James D. Sandy, Jr., and wife Alverta of Wilmington; daughter Kathy Warner and husband Ed Warner of Shippensburg, PA; grandchildren Eddie Warner of Oceanside, CA, Karl Warner of Frederick, MD, Jackie Jordan and husband Robert of Wilmington, James D. Sandy, III and wife Jana of Raleigh, NC; great-grandchildren Casie Warner of Oceanside, CA, Robert P. Jordan, III of Wilmington, NC, Chloe' R. Jordan of Wilmington, NC, and Ragan and Olivia Sandy of Raleigh, NC, and his beloved cat "Peanuts".

He and Dorothy enjoyed 27 years of traveling by motor home and traveled in Mexico, Canada and all states except Hawaii because Dorothy said there wasn't a bridge to get there.

He was a member of the Winter Park Baptist Church, and previously served as a deacon for a number of years starting in 1985 at the Harbor City Baptist Church in Melbourne, FL.

JD had the distinction of serving as a Frogman in WWII and was in the first NAVY UDT graduating class; which is the predecessor to the Navy Seals. He served in 12 invasion campaigns during the war. He retired from the Metropolitan Police Department in 1966 after 22 years of service.

He was Secretary Provost and served as Captain of the Motor Corps in the Almos Shrine Temple in Washington DC. After moving back to Wilmington in 1969, he remained active in the Shriners Drum and Bugle Corps, Sudan Temple, Wilmington and served as president of the Channel Haven Citizens Association. Over the years, he was also active in and held positions in the B.P.O. Elks and the American Legion in Wilmington.

Memorial services will be held 11 AM Saturday, May 21, 2011, at Winter Park Baptist Church.

Memorial contributions may be made to the Shriners Burn Centers, 3229 Burnett Ave., Cincinnatti, Ohio 45229.

Please share memories and condolences with the family at www.wilmingtoncares.com

Wilmington Funeral & Cremation, 1535 S. 41st Street, Wilmington, NC 28403; (910) 791-9099

In Memory of
John Noel Wilhide Jr.

December 22, 1924 - January 10, 1998

John passed away with family at his side January 10, 1998. Beloved husband of Lucy for 49 years. Loving father of John Phillip, Cynthia Ann, and Mark Richard. Proceeded in death by sons Noel Douglas, David Nelson. He will be missed by 10 grandchildren, and 13 great grandchildren.

John was born in the little town of Judson, North Carolina, to the proud parents of John and, Ethel Wilhide. In the mid-thirties the family moved to Swannanoa, North Carolina. He joined the Navy in 1943, and proudly served his country in WWII. He was in the first class of the Naval Combat Demolition Units. As a Gunner Mate 2nd class in NCDU #2 he was assigned to the Pacific Theater of the war.

After being discharged from the Navy he attended Warren Wilson College where he earned his degree in engineering. In 1948 he married Lucy Fulton, and together they had five children. In 1951 he moved to Michigan and started work with the Ford Motor Company. In 1960 he became a volunteer fire fighter in the City of Romulus. After retiring from Ford Motor Company, he became the first full time Fire Chief for the City of Romulus, and served the community for 22 years. John served on the Romulus Police, Fire and Safety Commission, and was very active in the city and his church. He will be missed by many family members and friends.

Funeral Services   Internment

St. Peter Lutheran Church   Michigan Memorial Park

Plymouth, Michigan   Flat Rock, Michigan

THE LAWTON CONSTITUTION

Samuel 'Sam' Pahdopony

Funeral for Samuel "Sam" Pahdopony, 85, Lawton, will be at 10 a.m. Saturday at Comanche Nation Funeral Home.

Mr. Pahdopony died Wednesday, Aug. 17, 2005.

Burial will be at Mount Scott KCA Cemetery.

He was born Sept. 22, 1919, to John and Mary Maddox Pahdopony. He married Marjorie Tahmahkera on March 15, 1940, in Lawton. He served in the U.S. Navy during World War II in the Pacific Theatre as one of the original "UDT/Frogmen," which later became the Navy Seals. He served in several campaigns in the Philippines, Admiralty Islands, Aitape, Biak, Noemfoor, New Guinea, Leyte, Mindoro, Lingayen Gulf, Zamboanaga, Talisay Cebu and Mindanao, Borneo, Tarakan and Brunei Bay.

Survivors include his wife, Lawton; a daughter and son-in-law, Juanita Pahdopony-Mithlo and Harry, Lawton; three grandchildren: Robert Hausman, Reno, Nev.; Brooke Corbett, Fort Worth, Texas; and Marc Hausman, Los Angeles; and a great-grandchild, Lauren Nicole Corbett.

He was preceded in death by his parents; and a brother, Howard Pahdopony.

Friends may call from 8 a.m. to 5 p.m. today at the funeral home.

Cemetery.

He was born Sept. 22, 1919, to John and Mary Maddox Pahdopony. He married Marjorie Tahmahkera on March 15, 1940, in Lawton. He served in the U.S. Navy during World War II in the Pacific Theatre as one of the original "UDT/Frogmen," which later became the Navy Seals. He served in several campaigns in the Philippines, Admiralty Islands, Aitape, Biak, Noemfoor, New Guinea, Leyte, Mindoro, Lingayen Gulf, Zamboanaga, Talisay Cebu and Mindanao, Borneo, Tarakan and Brunei Bay.

Survivors include his wife, Lawton; a daughter and son-in-law, Juanita Pahdopony-Mithlo and Harry, Lawton; three grandchildren: Robert Hausman, Reno, Nev.; Brooke Corbett, Fort Worth, Texas; and Marc Hausman, Los Angeles; and a great-grandchild, Lauren Nicole Corbett.

He was preceded in death by his parents; and a brother, Howard Pahdopony.

Friends may call from 8 a.m. to 5 p.m. today at the funeral home.

SAM PAHDOPONY 1945

SAM 1990

The Shooting of Buffalo From Barracks Windows is Prohibited.
by order of the COMMANDING OFFICER

206

When my dear friend Sam Pahdopony passed away, his wife sent me a statuette of a white Indian pony. I didn't understand the significance of it at first, so I did a little research.

Comanche warriors prepared for battle by painting their horses with various symbols of past victorious battles and of future successes. An Indian artist told me that the Comanche were a warrior people, who treasure their horses.

A Comanche's war pony was his brother in battle, the artist told me. He said, "When you ride him, he knows you and you know him and he's not going to default on you, He will never back out. When you are in a fight with a war pony, he is in there with you. He will never quit. He will die with you."

I think often of the men of Class 1, each one a war pony, each one my brother.

Photo courtesy John Valente

I am blessed to have had the opportunity to stand next to the greatest of men and to call them friends and brothers. Though my time in the Navy was short, it cast a long, bright glow over my whole life. The *Navy SEAL Ethos* talks about being "forged by adversity." I know we had plenty of that. Yet, adversity is not what endures in my heart. For me, what endures is the legacy of my teammates, the character and honor of good men whom I came to know well and to trust to the ends of this earth. They have steadied me in the worst moments, and our life-long bond sustains me to this day.

Hooyah!

www.PhocaPress.com
New York, NY 10025

Design and Layout: Lisa Merriam

Edited by Tom Hawkins and Lisa Merriam

We are grateful to Bruce Meberg who helped with the meticulous scanning
and cataloging of hundreds of images and delicate documents.

To Edward and Loretta Downey, we thank you for the support and publishing
expertise that has made this book possible.

Special thanks and Hooyah! to the National Navy UDT-SEAL Museum.

Phoca Press is pleased and honored that our first book presentation is by
one of the very first Naval Special Warfare operators. We began discussing at
length the importance of NSW's history and heritage, while collaborating on
portions of the Web site for the National Navy UDT-SEAL Museum. When
Bill approached us with his marvelous scrapbook, he gave us the impetus we
needed to start our company, and its focus on U.S. Navy SEAL and SWCC
operators and their legacy units. We thank Bill for giving us the very best of
reasons for forming Phoca Press. We sincerely hope Bill's book has started a
second legacy that does honor to his first.
— *Tom Hawkins and Lisa Merriam, Phoca Press Co-Founders*
February 13, 2015

CPSIA information can be obtained at www.ICGtesting.com
Printed in the USA
BVOW10*2108260515

401957BV00003B/3/P